Praise for *Inner City Renovation*

"Inner City Renovation is a compelling blend of from the field of urban regeneration, unde understanding of how policy can empower a... umcn communities when it takes account of both people and place. This book gives an insight into personal leadership, enterprising solutions and value creation, making it as relevant to practitioners engaged in social enterprise, urban regeneration and community empowerment as it is to policy makers and students with an interest in social responsibility."

— Gerry Higgins, Founder, Social Enterprise World Forum;
Chief Executive, Supporting Enterprise and Communities

"For some, social enterprise is a theoretical construct that has demonstrated potential for addressing community issues. Donkervoort goes beyond just the theoretical to capture the birth and maturing of a social enterprise that continues to make a difference to the inner-city residents lucky enough to be hired. *Inner City Renovation* is an inspiring record with the promise that more such enterprises will join a wave of development that considers people and community as important and reasonable profits."

— Wanda Wuttunee, Aboriginal Business
Education Program, University of Manitoba

"While reading *Inner City Renovation,* you'll share Donkervoort's personal journey through a changing culture of business — from the businesses based purely on profit of Bay Street to the social enterprise world where business is built on values to address the poverty of Winnipeg's Selkirk Avenue. Marty's book expertly explores the compelling, complex story of social enterprise, blending compassion and business … [and] addresses the realities of financing, managing and operating a social enterprise from concept through launch, growth and success."

—David LePage, Founding Member,
Social Enterprise Council of Canada

"It is so important to tell precise and fruitful stories about the beauty and challenges of [social enterprise] initiatives [that combine] economic relevance/viability with the quest for the public good. Marty Donkervoort does this with the talent of a professor living in the field he teaches and with the deep feelings and inspiration of a social entrepreneur who is ready to pay the price to help a community."

— Jacques Defourny, Director,
Centre for Social Economy, University of Liege

INNER CITY RENOVATION

INNER CITY RENOVATION

How a Social Enterprise Changes Lives and Communities

MARTY DONKERVOORT

Foreword by Jack Quarter

FERNWOOD PUBLISHING
HALIFAX & WINNIPEG

Editing and text design: Brenda Conroy
Cover design: John van der Woude
Cover photograph by Jerry Grajewski, Grajewski Fotograph. Inc.
Reprinted with permission of Jerry Grajewski.
All other photographs by the author.
Printed and bound in Canada by Hignell Book Printing

Published in Canada by Fernwood Publishing
32 Oceanvista Lane, Black Point, Nova Scotia, B0J 1B0
and 748 Broadway Avenue, Winnipeg, Manitoba, R3G 0X3
www.fernwoodpublishing.ca

Fernwood Publishing Company Limited gratefully acknowledges the financial support
of the Government of Canada through the Canada Book Fund and the Canada Council
for the Arts, the Nova Scotia Department of Communities, Culture and Heritage,
the Manitoba Department of Culture, Heritage and Tourism under the
Manitoba Publishers Marketing Assistance Program and the Province of Manitoba,
through the Book Publishing Tax Credit, for our publishing program.

Library and Archives Canada Cataloguing in Publication

Donkervoort, Marty, 1945-, author
Inner City Renovations: how a social enterprise changes lives and communities / Marty
Donkervoort.

Includes bibliographical references and index.
ISBN 978-1-55266-581-7 (pbk.)

1. Inner City Renovations. 2. Social entrepreneurship—Manitoba—Winnipeg. 3. Buildings—
Repair and reconstruction—Manitoba—Winnipeg. 4. Poor—Employment—Manitoba—
Winnipeg. 5. Community development—Manitoba—Winnipeg. 6. Social change—Manitoba—
Winnipeg. 7. Winnipeg (Man.)—Social conditions. I. Title.

HD60.5.C22W45 2013   361.2'509712743   C2013-902993-1

Contents

Acknowledgements

As this was my first experience at writing a book, I relied on support and assistance from many people. First of all I thank my spouse, Susan Prentice, for her support and encouragement not only while writing this book but also during the years I spent at Inner City Renovation. I am also grateful to her for creating the opportunity to spend a year in France upon my retirement from Inner City Renovation. It was a perfect transition from the challenging years as ICR's general manager to an unknown future. Being isolated in a new environment with time on my hands was ideal for writing about the experience that had consumed the last ten years of my life.

While living in France, I was fortunate to connect with Jacques Defourny, a professor of economics at University of Liege, Belgium, and director of the Centre d'Economie Sociele. The centre provided space and support, and I spent a week there working on the manuscript.

Upon my return to Canada, I discussed the manuscript with an old friend and colleague, Rebecca McKenzie, who assisted in developing a framework for the book. Thank you to Bill Young, Joanne Norris and Garry Loewen for reviewing and commenting on early draft sections of the manuscript. Thank you to Kaye Grant, Reconnaissance Management Consulting Group, for helping with the research for the book, and John Baker, my successor at ICR, for assisting with the postscript.

I am also thankful to my colleagues at the Social Enterprise Council of Canada, who have advanced the role of social enterprises in Canada and who over the years have inspired and supported me to do this work.

My sincere appreciation to Jack Quarter, professor and co-director of the Social Economy Centre at the Ontario Institute for Studies in Education, University of Toronto, for his inspiration both personally and through his books on the social economy. I am honoured and particularly grateful to him for taking time to write the foreword for this book.

I am indebted and forever grateful to the folks at Fernwood Publishing, especially Wayne Antony, whose guidance and patience was critical to completing this book. Also thanks to Brenda Conroy for copy editing the manuscript and designing the pages, Debbie Mathers for pre-production, Beverley Rach for production coordination and John van der Woude for the cover design.

Thanks also to the directors of Community Ownership Solutions and Inner City Renovation for their confidence in me and their support throughout my tenure. Most importantly, a huge thank you to all the ICR employees over the years, without whom there would be no story to tell. This book is dedicated to them.

Abbreviations

ACU	Assiniboine Credit Union
BUILD	Building Urban Industries for Local Development
CED	Centre for Community Enterprise
CEDA	Community Education Development Association
CEDNET	Canadian CED Network
CEO	Chief Executive Officer
CIC	community interest companies
COFI	Council of Forest Industries of British Columbia
COR	Certificate of Recognition
COS	Community Ownership Solutions
CPP	Canadian Pension Plan
CRS	Community Resources Systems
CUPE	Canadian Union of Public Employees
EMES	European Research Network
ENP	Enterprising Non Profits
FIRA	Foreign Investment Review Agency
GDP	gross domestic product
HOP	Housing Opportunity Partnership
HRDC	Human Resource Development Canada
ICD	Inner City Development
ICJ	Inner City Janitorial
ICPM	Inner City Property Management
ICR	Inner City Renovation
ILGWU	International Ladies Garment Workers Union
LEED	Leadership in Energy and Environmental Design
LTD	long-term disability
MCC	Mennonite Central Committee
MGEU	Manitoba Government Employees Union
MNHWP	Manitoba New Home Warranty Program
MYS	MacDonald Youth Services
NAFTA	North American Free Trade Agreement
NDP	New Democratic Party
NECRC	North End Community Renewal Corporation
NEHP	North End Housing Project
NGOs	non-government organizations
OPK	Ogijiita Pimatiswin Kinamatwin
PST	Provincial Sales Tax
RAY	Resource Assistance for Youth
SARC	Saskatchewan Association of Rehabilitation Centres
SCP	Social Capital Partners
SECC	Social Enterprise Council of Canada
SEED	Supporting Employment and Economic Development
SMEs	small and medium enterprises
SNA	Spence Neighbourhood Association
SRI	Social Responsible Investment
SROI	social return on investment
WBDC	West Broadway Development Corporation
WHRC	Winnipeg Housing and Rehab Corp
WODF	Worker Ownership Development Foundation

Foreword

Inner City Renovation: How a Social Enterprise Changes Lives and Communities is much more than the book title advertises: it is in fact three stories. First, it is an account of Inner City Renovation, the much-heralded social enterprise in Winnipeg, which has become an exemplar of the potential of social enterprises to rescue people living on the social margins and engage them in a productive livelihood. The second story is about the former general manager and board member of Inner City Renovation, Marty Donkervoort, and his fascinating journey from a relatively conventional career as the marketing manager in Noranda's forest products, with lots of money and the perks associated with large corporations, to one in which he channelled his energies to the development initially of worker cooperatives and subsequently of social enterprises. The third story in this book is about social enterprises in Canada and internationally and their potential.

The three stories, albeit distinct to a degree, are also one story, as the parts are interwoven. Inner City Renovation would not have come about without Marty Donkervoort's commitment and unusual pedigree for someone working in social enterprise of an MBA from the Schulich School of Business, York University. He not only believed in the social mission, as so many do, but also was able to apply his training towards ensuring that Inner City Renovation was on a sound business footing. Having a strong business plan has made it possible for Inner City Renovation to meet its social mission of gainful employment for persons on the social margins.

Similarly, Inner City Renovation is not simply an end in itself but a player in a social movement, which this book so successfully articulates, of organizations operating in the market that attempt to balance their business and social commitments. Donkervoort is clear in defining the parameters of this balance and the importance of the social enterprise movement in articulating this balance.

Inner City Renovation addresses the needs of people who operate on the margins of the labour market; the firm draws them into the workforce, not in high-paying jobs, but in employment that represents a major step forward for them and that utilizes their talents in producing and renovating houses, an important social contribution. This would not have occurred without a major investment of resources from a parent organization, Community Ownership Solutions, and from Social Capital Partners, which did much of the financing. There is a substantial cost to starting such enterprises, and from a business viewpoint, it is often the case that they don't break even. Many social enterprises rely upon government grants and supports from foundations. Yet, the costs must be balanced against the benefits, or what is often referred to as the "social return." In the case of Inner City Renovation, the social return is the employment of people, many of whom are of Aboriginal origin, who otherwise would be on various forms of social assistance or pensions and the associated personal benefits of gainful employment. This is a major accomplishment, which the book is able to articulate in a clear and unpretentious manner.

This book is important for anyone interested in starting a social enterprise, as the know-how of its author is informative, and for people who are interested in the field, as it is an inspiring feel-good story, which can only help with pushing forward the broader objective of creating a greater balance between business objectives of earning money and the objective of social betterment.

— Jack Quarter, Professor and Co-Director,
Social Economy Centre,
Ontario Institute for Studies in Education,
University of Toronto.

Preface

For almost ten years, I was involved, including as general manager for six years, in one of one of Canada's most successful social enterprises: Inner City Renovation in Winnipeg. I wrote this book out of exhilaration and inspiration. It was exhilarating to be involved from the ground up with an enterprise that has such a deep impact on its people and the community it is part of. The book, in part, documents the development ICR and those impacts. And, it was inspiring to see what a group of people, many of whom had been written off by much of society, can do when given opportunities within an alternative organization. So, I wrote this book to inspire others about the potential of social enterprise to make a different kind of society.

On a more personal level, writing this book was a transition to a new phase of my life, a transition from day-to-day operational management to teaching, writing, speaking and consulting about social enterprise. All of these new activities are part of my desire to share the experience gained while working in the social economy and specifically in the development and management of a social enterprise. Since I started writing this book, I have developed and taught a course on social enterprise in both the Faculty of Business and the Urban and Inner Studies Department at the University of Winnipeg. I have also co-authored a case study on ICR, delivered presentations and workshops on social enterprise throughout Canada, and worked as a consultant to organizations in the social enterprise/social economy sector. The life journey that prepared me for and brought me to this stage is long and diverse.

In this book, I describe and reflect on the development, learning and outcomes of ICR from its pre start-up phase in 2001 to my departure in mid 2010. ICR continues to thrive to this day. It has maintained its commitment to the social mission while doubling its revenue and improving its profitability.

This story about ICR, in large part, focuses on the key nuts-and-bolts issues for a social enterprise. The legal, financial, governance and marketing related to the development and sustainability of social enterprises, which are identified and elaborated on, are complex and often counter-intuitive. Governments do play a key role, and relevant governmental policies are important for organizations in this sector. However, in this respect, there are both opportunities and dangers for social enterprises.

While the story of the inputs, activities and outcomes associated with ICR are important and interesting, most important is documenting the impacts Inner City Renovation has on its employees and on the community. Working at ICR is vastly different from working in the corporate capitalist sector of our economy. The personal journeys of ICR's employees are the heart of this part of the story. My own journey, included at the urging of social enterprise colleagues, tells of my transition from a high-powered corporate career to the social economy. This part of the ICR story shows the significance of social justice values to the success of a social enterprise. The whole ICR story is a reflection on the challenges and benefits of a social enterprise in a stressed community and a tribute to the ingenuity and dedication of its employees.

To put it briefly and bluntly, social enterprises are real businesses selling goods or services to real customers; they compete, and must compete, in the marketplace. Too often, social enterprises are driven only by social justice values. To be successful, they must also be real economic organizations. Yet, the way they fit into their communities, the dignity and respect with which they treat their employees and their goal of moving toward social justice and equality signify that they truly represent an alternative to corporate capitalism.

As will be evident already, I am an insider and participant in the ICR story. I developed the business concept, wrote the business plan, participated as a board member and ultimately managed the enterprise. This had its advantages in writing this book, as I am very familiar with all of the events related to the enterprise and intimately familiar with many of the employees' lives. The downside of this intimacy is that it could have led me to be somewhat less than objective. At times I may have been too enthusiastic in my evaluation of the impact of ICR on people's lives and on the local community and of the potential of social enterprise. For any such overzealousness, I apologize; yet, I am hopeful that it provides insight as well.

In the end, the book shows that a relatively small social enterprise can illuminate a way forward where traditional capitalist responses to poverty and social exclusion do not. Social enterprise can change people's lives, renew communities and, ultimately, create a more equal and just society.

Part I

THE SOCIAL ENTERPRISE

Chapter 1

Set Up and Management

Inner City Renovation (ICR) is a Winnipeg-based general contractor in the construction sector. The enterprise started operations on August 1, 2002, providing renovation services to several inner city not-for-profit community organizations. These organizations provided affordable and safe housing for inner city low-income families. Since then, ICR has expanded its services to constructing new buildings in both the residential and commercial sectors. It has also expanded in the private market while continuing its role in the not-for-profit sector. By mid 2010, ICR had completed more than 125 projects, with an associated earned revenue of more than $10 million.

Role Played by Community Ownership Solutions

In the late 1990s, the Crocus Investment Fund, created by the Manitoba Federation of Labour, wanted to assist in the alleviation of poverty in Winnipeg's inner city, particularly in the North End. After much consultation with social economy activists across North America, a not-for-profit organization called Community Ownership Solutions (COS) was incorporated in 1999. Its specific mandate was to create quality jobs for inner city residents who were unemployed and/or on social assistance. Quality jobs were defined as those that paid market or better wages, provided health and other benefits, included education and training, had opportunities for career advancement, existed within a participative management culture and provided an opportunity for employee ownership. This last point that was important in choosing the legal structure for subsequent social enterprises because only share capital corporations (for profit) can allocate or sell ownership shares to its employees.

COS founding members Sherman Kreiner (President and CEO, Crocus Investment Fund), Doug Davison (Vice President, Crocus Investment Fund) and Jan Lederman (a corporate lawyer with Thompson Dorfman and Sweatman) set out to develop a plan to recruit board members and raise funds. It was decided that the board should include key individuals from business, labour, educational institutes and community organizations. Board recruitments included David Friesen (Friesen Corporation), Bob Chipman (Megill- Stephenson Company Limited), Paul Moist (CUPE), Stan Bear (Romanow, Bear and Associates), Constance Rooke (University of Winnipeg), Anita Stenning (City of Winnipeg), Drew Cringan (McKim Communication), Ted Jackson (Carlton University), Garry Loewen (North End Community Renewal Corporation) and Carolyn Rodgers (Assiniboine Credit Union).

The Crocus Investment Fund provided in-kind services, including management advice, office space, access to photocopiers, telephone and internet, to support COS in its initial development. The founders of COS approached the Charles Stewart Mott Foundation in Flint, Michigan, for funding. The Foundation's vision is a world in which each of us is in partnership with the rest of the human race — where each individual's quality of life is connected to the well-being of the community, both locally and globally. Sherman Kreiner was well known to the Mott Foundation, and the initiative received its first grant prior to COS's incorporation as a legal entity. I started as COS general manager in December 2001.

COS's goal to create quality jobs for inner city low-income residents was to be pursued in a two ways: by supporting existing enterprises and by developing new enterprises. COS first entered into several fee-for-service contracts with private enterprises in an effort to improve the quality of their jobs. This was seen and pitched as a win-win situation for both the employees and the employer: better wages, benefits and job satisfaction for the employees and, resulting from a happier workforce, improved productivity and reduced turnover (resulting in fewer recruitment and training costs) for the employer. At the same time, COS was conducting feasibility studies with a view to starting up its own enterprise. The enterprise creation strategy was pursued so that COS would be able to create quality jobs without having to persuade existing business owners to change their hiring policies and management styles.

Pre Start-Up Planning (2000–2002)

COS explored opportunities in several sectors, including security, janitorial and temporary work. After a year of market research and a number of feasibility studies, COS identified an opportunity to start an enterprise in the construction/renovation sector. There were numerous derelict houses in Winnipeg's inner city and at the same time a housing shortage, especially for low-income families. These factors pointed to an opportunity for an enterprise that could address both unemployment and lack of adequate housing in the North End. Several not-for-profit community housing organizations had already been set up to address the housing shortage. These organizations were dependent on private for-profit contractors for renovation services. The model being developed by COS was holistic in that it would not only provide employment and training but also renovation services for these community not-for-profit housing organizations. It integrated these two inner city realities into one approach rather than having them compete with each other for scarce funding. The proposed model would capitalize on the demand for inner city housing renewal and incorporate job creation for people that are typically outside the labour force. This was especially important as the largely unskilled inner city population was increasing and the traditional skilled labour force was decreasing.

As part of the feasibility study, four inner city not-for-profit community organizations involved in social housing — North End Housing Project (NEHP), Winnipeg Housing and Rehab Corp (WHRC), Spence Neighbourhood Association (SNA) and West Broadway Development Corporation (WBDC) — were asked if they were interested in being part of an enterprise that would provide renovation services while employing community residents, some of whom were already residing in their houses or were potential tenants.

Having received a positive interest from these organizations to the proposal, I drafted a business plan for the enterprise. The executive summary of this plan is included in Appendix 1. With a comprehensive business plan for the enterprise in hand, I met with the boards of directors and senior staff of these community organizations to solicit their commitment. All four organizations agreed to support the enterprise and to become shareholders.

I became aware of a business plan competition, sponsored by Social Capital Partners (SCP) in Toronto, for social enterprises addressing employment issues in low-income communities. Bill Young, a social entrepreneur interested in supporting non-traditional enterprises in the social economy, had recently set up SCP. This organization was offering $15,000 in cash and up to a million dollars in financing as well as technical and management support to the enterprise with the winning business plan. Our business plan was submitted, and it won. Much later, I found out that more than a hundred plans from across Canada had been submitted to the competition.

In June 2002, Inner City Renovation was incorporated with six shareholders: the four inner city development corporations (NEHP, WHRC, SNA, WBDC), along with SCP and COS. All were not-for-profits and all, with the exception of SCP, had charitable status. Each shareholder bought ten shares valued at one dollar each. COS and SCP provided $215,000 start-up capital as well as the management support services for the new enterprise. The community housing developers in turn agreed to provide a certain percentage of their renovation work to the newly formed social enterprise. These and other terms were spelled out in a shareholders agreement signed by all the participants. Each of the shareholders was permitted to appoint one director to the ICR board. While the majority of board and policy decisions were decided democratically, certain financial decisions as well as issues dealing with dissolution of the enterprise required the explicit approval of COS and SCP. As ICR was not intended to be a sheltered workplace or a conventional training centre, it incorporated as a for-profit share capital corporation. This structure allowed for the possibility of employee ownership, considered an important criterion for a quality job. Perhaps more importantly, it installed an expectation for employees that the success of the enterprise was in large part dependent on their commitment. It also prepared employees for transitioning to other employers in the industry should they decide to leave ICR.

Early Start-Up Years (2002–2004)

ICR started up operations as a general construction contractor on August 1, 2002. The enterprise provided a complete range of construction services with its own labour force and with sub-contracting services such as concrete foundations, roofing, electrical, plumbing and mechanical. At start-up, ICR had commitments for more than a million dollars in renovation work from its community organization shareholders and up to a million dollars of potential financing in grants and loans from SCP and COS.

COS shared its ground floor office at the Crocus Building in downtown Winnipeg with ICR. David Elson was ICR's first general manager and Cheryl Lisoway its first office manager. Both had been employed prior to the start-up date to set up the office, draft operational procedures, hire staff and negotiate contracts. The first ten crew employees all came from Just Housing, a carpentry training program set up by Community Education Development Association (CEDA) in Winnipeg's North End. A skilled journeyperson carpenter was hired to lead the crews.

COS had received funding from Manitoba's Department of Intergovernmental Affairs and the Winnipeg Foundation to implement and support its social enterprise job creation program. COS used this funding to invest in ICR and trigger the SCP matching funds. As a new start-up with little or no equity, ICR was not in a position to obtain loans from traditional financial institutions. ICR negotiated a $150,000 credit line with Assiniboine Credit Union (ACU) to finance cash flow. The Crocus Investment Fund continued to provide support with in-kind services that included staff secondment and administrative services. In addition, SCP staff members Sean Van Doorselaer and Joanne Norris made numerous trips to Winnipeg to provide assistance with financial management and

ICR staff putting finishing touches on a renovation in Spence neighbouhood

Urban Circle Training Centre on Selkirk Avenue in Winnipeg's North End

support for its social mission. Sean helped with refinements to the business plan, financial modeling and identifying new market opportunities, and Joanne assisted with governance and staffing issues. Joanne also developed the social return on investment analysis for ICR. As an ICR board member, Bill Young made numerous trips to Winnipeg to provide valuable insights and support to me personally. He also participated in monthly telephone management meetings to review performance and chart ICR's course during the difficult start-up period. SCP's involvement provided moral support to ICR management.

During its first year, ICR concentrated on renovations for the shareholder community housing organizations mainly in Winnipeg's North End. These were labour intensive, as the houses were stripped to their basic shells and rebuilt, and relatively simple, as the renovations were without any frills. As a contractor in the residential market, ICR took out a membership in the Manitoba Home Builders' Association and in the Better Business Bureau.

Before the first year was up, ICR pursued an opportunity to enter the commercial renovation market as contractors for the Urban Circle Training Centre on Selkirk Avenue in Winnipeg's North End. The conversion of an old and dilapidated Woolworths store to a modern Aboriginal training school was a challenge. ICR had to take on more skilled staff, as the project was more complex than the simple residential home renovation it was used to. ICR completed the project on time and as per the architect's specifications. It did, however, take a significant loss on the project, partially due to estimating errors but also because of the learning curve for everyone, from crew members to supervisors to management, related to taking on a large complex project.

Urban Circle Training Centre interior

As ICR entered the commercial market, the role of unions was discussed. Up to that point, it had not been an issue as the residential renovation sector is dominated by small enterprises with a few employees and is not unionized. However, the commercial construction sector has a significant union presence. From the outset, ICR had been supported by organized labour, and the labour movement wanted to support progressive initiatives, especially employment creation related to poverty reduction. It was also supportive of ICR's commitment to apprenticeship training. During my tenure in the general management position, while on secondment from the Crocus Investment Fund, I was a member of the Manitoba Government Employees Union (MGEU). There was, however, never any pressure to organize ICR's employees, nor did the employees express a desire to join a union to protect their individual rights.

Although ICR's financial performance was very poor in its start-up years, it did very well towards achieving its social goals. More than twenty jobs were created with good wages and health benefits. Social supports were provided, and social activities and celebrations were organized. Employees were treated with respect and dignity. Its early experiences resulted in the following changes to ICR's social goals and business plan:

- The minimum level of employees from low-income inner city residents was reduced from 70 to 60 percent.
- The ratio of skilled workers and trainees to one skilled (preferably jour-

neyperson) worker was reduced from five or six to three or less.

- With the realization that dealing with the social-related issues of staff was time consuming and difficult, ICR contracted a trained social worker from the community to provide assistance to its employees.
- Due to the irregular timing of renovation contracts from its shareholders, ICR realized that it had to diversify its client base in order to have sufficient work on an ongoing basis to maintain its workforce without layoffs.
- Realizing that crew supervisors needed to be more sympathetic and accommodating to the realities of the workforce, ICR coached supervisors on personnel issues, including showing up for work on time, ready and able to work, as well as on motivating and training staff.
- Management, particularly the general manager, had a difficult role balancing the social and financial bottom lines while also delivering projects on time and on budget. The board decided to search for a new general manager better suited to the complexities of this role.

At the same time that ICR was starting up, COS was still pursuing its other quality job strategy with private enterprises in several other sectors. This work was being funded by Western Economic Diversification Canada, a department of the federal government committed to strengthening western innovation, business development and community economic development. This dual approach continued, but by the end of 2003, COS focused its full resources on the new enterprise job creation strategy.

Growing Pains (2004–2005)

ICR started this period with a new general manager, as the board struggled to get the right balance between technical construction and business management experience and compassionate human resource skills in the general manager position. ICR was also adjusting to the complexities of commercial renovations, which now represented approximately half of the work. During this period, three of the four not-for-profit housing development shareholders decided to pull out. New management at WHRC decided to go with private contractors, and SNA, which was dependent on WHRC for its housing construction program, left with them. The West Broadway Neighbourhood was running out of dilapidated houses to renovate. ICR continued with its three (COS, SCP and NEHP) remaining shareholders while diversifying its client base in the private residential sector.

ICR continued to incur annual financial losses during this period. Although NEHP provided a large volume of work, approximately twenty house renovations per year representing more than a million dollars in annual revenue, the margins associated with this work were too low and were not sufficient to cover ICR's overhead costs.

Throughout this period, ICR also struggled to combat theft and vandalism. It seemed that a month could not go by without a break-in on one of its jobsites. On one occasion, ICR crew arriving in the morning at a jobsite in the Point Douglas Neighbourhood discovered that the entire shipment of doors and moldings that had been delivered late the previous day had been stolen. This theft included material that had already been installed. With the increase in the price of copper, no project was safe from copper theft, with thieves cutting out new lines that had already been installed. Tools too were easy prey for thieves, even while workers were on-site but out of sight. Shortly after start-up, ICR purchased a number of large theft-proof metal toolboxes to combat theft. This strategy was given up when thieves carried out the entire toolbox during an after-hours break-in. As a result of these experiences all tools and equipment were returned to ICR's shop at the end of each workday and locked up. Delivery of materials was limited to those that could be installed during the workday, thus reducing the likelihood of theft. All of these precautions resulted in increased costs related to transportation and downtime on job sites while awaiting material and equipment deliveries.

It was also during this period in ICR's evolution that it started to negotiate cost-plus contracts instead of fixed-price contracts. ICR had survived several huge losses related to fixed-price contracts and realized that another significant loss could put it out of business. Cost-plus contracts were based on trust; overhead and profit margins were agreed upon at the outset, and invoices and internal company records documented costs. Cost-plus contracts guarded against potential losses on projects and at the same time provided flexibility to customers, as renovations were often full of unforeseen surprises, which in fixed-price contracts triggered expensive change orders.

Participation in the tendering process to acquire contracts, which is usual in the construction sector as well as with government procurement, also presented difficulties to ICR. Tenders are usually awarded to the lowest bidder, which might be okay for the purchaser but it tends to squeeze the margins for the provider of the goods or service. Another reason for shying away from tenders was that most major contracts required both a bid bond as proof of viability and, if awarded, a performance bond, which provided the customers with insurance in case the contractor defaulted. It is extremely difficult for social enterprises to qualify for bonding, as bonding agencies require a minimum level of equity on the company's balance sheet. ICR applied for and was turned down by traditional bonding agencies.

Transition Years (2006–2008)

After three general managers in ICR's first four years, COS seconded me to take on direct responsibility of ICR as its fourth general manager. Up to that point, I had been a director on ICR's board and provided management support services, including funding, marketing, sales and human resources.

In December of 2005, Inner City Renovation Inc. changed its legal name to Inner City Development Inc. (ICD) to accommodate the start-up of two new social enterprises, Inner City Janitorial (ICJ) and Inner City Property Management (ICPM). The construction enterprise ICR continued to operate as a division of ICD along with ICJ and ICPM. All three enterprises operated out of the joint ICR/COS office space, which had moved to Winnipeg's North End in 2003. Management staff with experience in janitorial services and property management was hired to start up these two divisions. Both division managers now reported to me as ICD's general manager, while I also continued in my role as general manager responsible for ICR (ICD's construction division).

COS had been looking for new opportunities to start up additional social enterprises. Thus, when a number of community organizations suggested that there was a demand for these two services, COS conducted feasibility studies that confirmed a need. It was thought that the three services would provide a synergy, with ICPM passing on work to both ICR for maintenance and renovation work and to ICJ for janitorial services. In addition, the three enterprises could share staff as required to fulfill contractual obligations. ICJ was able to negotiate a number of janitorial contracts, which included a financial institution, a school and several community organizations. Contracts required services to be provided seven days a week, mainly in the evening hours. ICJ participated in a number of government tenders, which if successful would have provided the required critical mass to make the enterprise viable. On each tender, ICJ was the high bidder, with a bid that was sometimes more than double that of the winner. Upon close examination of the tender guidelines and analysis of the winning bids, I determined that they were not based on paying workers legislated minimum wages. The norm in the sector is for contractors to employ workers on self-employed contracts, thus circumventing minimum wage standards. With a commitment to fair wages and benefits, ICJ could not compete in this environment and obtain the critical mass necessary to sustain itself. It ceased operations once its existing contracts expired in May 2007.

ICPM was set up in response to a number of community non -profit organizations that owned and managed properties with existing staff, who were often not familiar with property management. ICPM concentrated on the commercial market, as it did not want to compete with not-for-profit property managers in the residential sector. ICPM started with five contracts in the commercial sector and an expectation that others would follow. As 2006 progressed, it was unable to negotiate any new contracts. In addition, most of the existing clients were facing financial cutbacks and decided they could not afford the 5 percent management fee. They did not renew their annual contracts and reverted to using their own management staff for property management functions. ICPM closed its doors in December 2006, exactly one year after its start-up. Although the original premise of synergy between the three enterprises was valid, the two new enterprises could not obtain enough business to make them viable. ICD continued its operations with ICR as the sole operating division.

By July 31, 2007 — year five — the financial situation at ICR had reached a crisis point. This prompted the COS board to concentrate all of its efforts and resources on ICR. As one COS board member put it, "we are betting the house" on this new approach. It would either turn ICR around, or both COS and

Infill house complete; ground floor doors and windows remain boarded up till the house is occupied.

ICR would shut down. A number of significant events happened during this transition period. In mid 2007, NEHP ceased active operations after a power struggle between NEHP's board and staff. The ICR shares held by NEHP were returned in December of that year, and ICR continued on with only two key shareholders (COS and SCP). The loss of the NEHP revenue and the volume of work it represented were critical and had to be replaced. The silver lining for ICR was that work on new private residential and commercial projects had higher profit margins than the previous residential renovation work for its shareholders.

During this period, ICR also entered the residential new construction market. It acquired R2000 certification, an energy efficiency standard administered by the province, and joined the Manitoba New Home Warranty Program (MNHWP), both of which were prerequisites to participate in the city's infill housing program. The membership in the MNHWP program required $30,000, to be held on deposit with the program. SCP and COS provided the funds on an equal basis for the MNHWP deposit.

ICR also started constructing new buildings in the commercial sector. A number of large commercial projects were completed during this transition period, including two new branches for Assiniboine Credit Union and a number of large projects for Southern Authority Child and Family Services. ICR built a trusting relationship with several architects. It also developed closer relationships with its subcontractors (plumbing, electrical, mechanical and concrete). In addition, it developed relationships with other larger general contractors that provided construction services as subcontractors.

At this point in time other organizations and agencies started to support ICR. The new Winnipeg Partnership Agreement, a partnership between three levels of government to revitalize Winnipeg neighbourhoods, provided a large multi-year grant, and the Manitoba government education and training program continued to provide an annual training subsidy in the amount of $50,000. In 2006, the United Way of Winnipeg, a community organization committed to creating opportunities for a better life for everyone, started to support ICR with annual grants. The Co-operators Community Economic Development Fund, whose purpose is to support community enterprises and initiatives that create local employment and promote local self-reliance, also began to provide annual grants to ICR via COS to support training and social supports. This was part of these two organizations' commitment to supporting the social enterprise sector. By year six, ICR approached The Co-operators insurance company, which had been very supportive to ICR over the years, and it agreed to provide bonding facilities up to a maximum of $750,000.

During this period there were a number of changes at the COS board of directors. New directors, including Lloyd Axworthy, President, University of Winnipeg, Josie Hill, Co-director, Ma Mawi Wi Chi Itata Centre, Mike

Assiniboine Credit Union Rivergrove Branch on north Main Street under construction

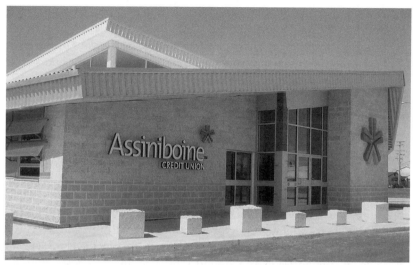

Assiniboine Credit Union Rivergrove Branch on north Main Street completed

Rattray, partner, MMP Architects, Dennis Lewycky, Communication Director, Canadian Union of Public Employees (CUPE) and Cheryl Crowe, Social Responsible Investment (SRI) Specialist, Assiniboine Credit Union (ACU) joined the board to replace departing members. Paul Moist, Carolyn Rodgers and Constance Rooke had left Winnipeg and therefore resigned from the board, while others, including David Friesen, Jan Lederman, Anita Stenning and Ted Jackson, left due to time commitments. A core of five founding directors continued throughout this period.

By 2007, shortly after NEHP became inactive, ICR entered into a relationship with the Housing Opportunity Partnership (HOP), a not-for-profit inner city housing revitalization initiative dedicated to reclaiming houses, streets and neighbourhoods by acquiring homes in need of repair, completely upgrading them and then selling them to new homeowners. The Winnipeg Realtors Association initiated HOP, and ICR became the sole contractor for its social housing program, providing both renovation services and new houses under the infill housing program. This relationship was similar to the one ICR had with NEHP although not at the same volume. ICR started to receive recognition for its role and its achievements. In 2008, the Manitoba Apprenticeship and Certification Board chose ICR as the "Provincial Employer of the Year." ICR also won a provincial sustainability award in the same year.

Later Years (2009–2010)

As it turns out the strategy implemented by COS in 2006 was successful. By 2010 (year eight), ICR had eliminated the accumulated deficit and created a small surplus. ICR had replaced the NEHP revenue with new revenue with higher profit margins. Social mission objectives were never sacrificed during the crisis and the road to profitability.

In these later years, ICR and its employees earned various distinctions. Charity Intelligence Canada, an organization committed to help donors make informed and intelligent giving decisions that can have the greatest impact for Canada, recognized ICR as one of four social enterprises in Canada to support. An ICR journey carpenter and crew supervisor was nominated for Manitoba journeyperson of the year and chosen as runner-up in a competition that included all trades.

ICR was engaged in a variety of projects, which included the Ahsanook project for the Southern First Nation Network of Care. This project renovated what used to be a convent into a care centre for Aboriginal youth. Phase one was completed in 2009, and work on phase two continued into 2010. In July 2009, a major renovation project for MacDonald Youth Services at its head office building led to a relationship whereby ICR became the contractor of choice for its properties in and around Winnipeg. In 2010, just before my departure, ICR had entered into a contract to renovate the Winnipeg Realtors three-storey office building on Portage Avenue.

As ICR became profitable during this period, it started distributing some of the profit to its employees. Although these profit distributions were relatively small, the process sent a message to its employees that the company was committed to profit distribution resulting from their labour and commitment.

By 2010, after an eight-year wonderful relationship as ICR shareholder and supporter, SCP redeemed its shares in ICR to pursue other projects, leaving COS as the only shareholder in ICR.

Management Succession in 2010

Starting in early 2009, I communicated to the COS and ICR boards my decision to leave in the spring of 2010. For years my family and I planned to take a year abroad during one of my spouse's sabbaticals in her work as an academic, and 2010, coinciding with my sixty-fifth birthday and our kids' transition year in their schools, seemed like the perfect opportunity. Succession planning started soon thereafter, with funding proposals to various foundations to assist in the succession-related expenses. A total of $40,000 had been estimated as necessary to assist with recruitment and salary expenses during a three-month overlap period. The Winnipeg Foundation, which had been helpful during the start-up years, agreed to provide the necessary funds.

Recruitment started in late 2009. Articles regarding the ICR succession were circulated and printed in community economic development journals and newsletters. The Centre for Community Enterprise, publisher of the CED magazine *Making Waves*, sent a personal email to all of its contacts across Canada to assist in the search for a successor. ICR board members assisted with the search among their contacts. Michelle Manary, a professional human resource specialist, offered to assist in the executive search on a pro bono basis. Ads were also placed in local and national newspapers. The search generated thirty applications, and eight were shortlisted as possible candidates.

The ideal candidate needed to possess both management and technical experience as well as strong leadership abilities and sensitivity to social issues. This was a tall order. Applicants included architects and engineers, some of whom had business training. There were also several young applicants just finishing their MBAs who had little or no work experience. Not surprisingly none of the applicants had ever managed a social enterprise or any enterprise with multiple bottom lines. The succession committee consisted of one ICR board member, the human resource specialist and me as the outgoing general manager. By mid-March, the committee had not been able to find a suitable successor to start by the June 1 deadline.

Dennis Lewycky, the ICR board chair and member on the succession committee, renewed his offer to take on the general manager role on an interim basis until a new permanent person could be found. Dennis was familiar with the organization, having spent one of his summer vacations volunteering at ICR. He was also on the verge of leaving his position with a national labour union. This gave the organization and the succession committee some breathing room.

Bill Young, ICR shareholder and board member, mentioned ICR's succession difficulties to John Baker over lunch in Toronto. To Bill's surprise, John indicated that he was interested in the position. Bill communicated John's interest to the committee, which approached him to set up an interview. John was well known to many people in the social enterprise and community economic development sectors. As well as being a partner in a successful management consulting company, he also developed and taught a social enterprise course at the York University Shullitz Business School in Toronto. John had had a long career in the Canadian navy, where he had both managed people and gained technical construction expertise.

John was interested in the position and the challenge it presented. The committee felt that John had the necessary credentials and commitment to take on the ICR management position. After several discussions, both parties agreed to a two-month trial period, at the end of which either party could decide to proceed or not. The trial period benefitted both sides; it would give ICR, both board and staff, a chance to see John in the management role, and it would allow John to get better acquainted with the many challenges inherent in the position. Over the next two months, John made a number of trips to Winnipeg staying a week at a time and returning to Toronto on weekends. By mid June, both parties were ready to sign an agreement that would see John take on the general manager position on a full-time basis by mid July. He continued to work with Dennis Lewycky to provide the necessary management from the time I left at the end of May.

Highlights of ICR's Development During the Period 2002–2010

Social Goals

As part of its social mission, ICR created more than thirty full-time, year-round quality jobs. All aspects of a quality job outlined by COS, including wages and benefits, training, democratic participatory workplace and opportunities for advancement, were achieved during this period.

Operational Goals

ICR met its operational goals, acquiring space and equipment necessary to carry out its operations. It hired management staff and developed relationships with suppliers, contractors and architects. ICR managed to survive the challenges of the early start-up period and developed into a sustainable enterprise delivering services to both commercial and residential clients.

Financial Goals

Although it took much longer to reach financial stability than initially projected, ICR broke even in 2006 and eliminated accumulated deficits by 2009. Upon my departure in 2010, ICR had just completed its most profitable year and was debt free. That same year more than 95 percent of ICR's revenue was earned from construction contracts. The remaining 5 percent came from grants to support training.

ICR's Uniqueness

ICR's incorporation as a for-profit enterprise with not-for-profit shareholders is different from most social enterprises, which either operate as part of a not-for-profit organization or as an independent not-for-profit. ICR's relationship with COS, a registered charity committed to poverty alleviation, is also unique, allowing charitable funds to be used for creating and supporting employment in a stressed community. ICR's relationships with the labour movement, the local Aboriginal community and Winnipeg's corporate sector are all somewhat unique for a social enterprise. ICR was an early participant in Leadership in Energy and Environmental Design (LEED) certified construction projects in Winnipeg including the Mountain Equipment Co-op building in downtown Winnipeg and a new branch for Assiniboine Credit Union in the south part of Winnipeg. Being recognized as the Employer of the Year in 2008 by the Manitoba Apprenticeship and Certification Board was very special and unique, since ICR was selected from all companies in all sectors in Manitoba.

Part 2

**WORKING AT
INNER CITY RENOVATION**

Chapter 2

Changing Employees' Lives

"Building inner-city hope one vital job at a time" —*Winnipeg Free Press*, May 2, 2009

Most of ICR's employees have a long history in Winnipeg's inner city, a history that includes living in substandard housing, spotty or no employment, inadequate nutrition, poor health, interpersonal strife and violence. These are not great backgrounds from which to draw the personal resources to maintain steady and productive employment.

In the late 1990s, housing in the inner city was dismal. Years of neglect had taken their toll. Broken windows, leaky roofs and faulty plumbing created damp and mouldy living conditions, which seriously affected the health of the occupants.[1] Absentee landlords, it would seem, saw no need to invest in the properties, especially in a tight rental accommodation market. The vacancy rate in all of Winnipeg in 2002 was 1.1 percent, and it was less than 0.5 percent for units with low rents.[2] People fortunate enough to have a place to live put up with the poor living conditions, and in 2002 people living in public housing didn't fare much better.

The inner city was dotted with sleazy hotels where rooms rented by the night or week. Although these also tended to be dismal places, they were often preferred to shelters run by community or religious organizations, which required residents to vacate the premises daily.

Many of the inner city neighbourhoods were unsafe, particularly at night when gangs take over ownership of their territories. Young men with little prospect of employment were lured into gangs.[3] This was the environment in which many of ICR's employees found themselves at the time ICR started up in 2002. By creating employment opportunities and providing improved housing conditions, ICR was trying to make a significant and lasting change in the conditions of inner city neighbourhoods and their residents.

Employment Creation

As the Ecumenical Coalition for Economic Justice stated: "Unemployment has been the single most reliable predictor of poverty for those aged 18–65."[4] Consequently, as part of its role in addressing poverty, ICR made employment creation one of its main goals. More than 120 people were employed by ICR during the eight-year span between August 2002 and August 2010. Full-time staff increased over this period from twelve to thirty. There is a relatively high turnover rate, mainly at the entry level since recruitment is based on providing opportunities to those wanting to obtain employment. Local community-based employment agencies assist with screening candidates to determine whether potential employees are able and ready to take on full-time employment. Even with this screening process, success is still related to the employee's ability to adjust to full-time work in the construction sector. New employees realize very quickly whether or not they are ready for construction work. In some cases, management has to step in and let go some employees who are unable to adjust.

Many of the new recruits have a long history of unemployment and social assistance. For some, this is related to a lack of technical skills and work experience; for others, difficulties in finding employment are related to mental health issues or addictions. Criminal records are another obstacle preventing some from obtaining employment. A number are trying to leave a gang-related life and make a new start. Most of the people employed by ICR have encountered significant difficulties in finding and maintaining employment in private sector companies due to these various circumstances, which give rise to problems that most businesses will not tolerate at all. ICR's support system for entry-level employees from the inner city environment differentiate it from other companies claiming job creation initiatives.

Because the population of Winnipeg's inner city neighbourhoods includes up to 40 percent First Nations, more than 50 percent of the new ICR recruits are Aboriginal. ICR is committed to hiring at least 60 percent of its employees from the inner city, low-income population. Originally at 70 percent, this figure was reduced to 60 percent in the second year to balance ICR's skilled to non-skilled worker ratio. The 60 percent level has been maintained since then.

Wages

Low wages are an undisputed cause of persistent poverty in Canada.[5] During the first eight years, ICR paid out more than $3 million in wages and benefits to its employees. The minimum wage for an ICR entry-level position, which requires little or no experience or skills, was $8 per hour in 2002 and increased to $11 per hour by 2010. This compared favourably with the provincial minimum wage levels, which were $6.50 in 2002 and $9.50 by 2010. Supervisory staff, usually journeypersons, had the highest wages, in line with the industry average rate of $22 to $25 per hour by 2010. The average wage rate for all employees at ICR in 2002 was $13.50 per hour, which increased to $19.25 per hour by 2010. The high turnover rate at ICR, which starts new people at the lower wage rates, has the effect of keeping the average wage rate lower than would be expected, since there are always new entry-level employees at the lower wage rate.

In 2010, the ratio of top management earnings to the average worker at ICR was 2.5:1, and only 3:1 compared to the lowest paid worker. This is a far cry from norms in the construction sector, or any other sector for that matter, where ratios are 10:1 or higher. Ratios as high as 500:1 have been documented in large North American Corporations.[6] In the immediate short term, this low ratio was important towards creating a more equal workplace, and over the longer term it contributed to creating a more equal community. Social equality leads to improved health, better housing, less violence, reduced crime, lower incarceration rates, fewer teenage pregnancies and a sense of well-being that affects everyone in the community, not just the disadvantaged.[7]

In the early years, wages were paid bi-weekly by cheque. Most of the employees did not have bank accounts, and the few that did needed to travel out of the neighbourhood, as there were no longer any financial institutions located in the city core, where most of the employees lived. Consequently, paycheques were usually cashed at local cheque-cashing businesses, such as Money Mart, which charge a considerable fee for their services. In 2004, ICR started an automatic payroll deposit system whereby pay was deposited directly into the employee's bank account. ICR management assisted employees to open up accounts with Assiniboine Credit Union (ACU), which allows them to withdraw cash at any ATM machine, thereby circumventing the usurious cheque-cashing charges.

Health Benefits

From day one, ICR has been committed to providing a full range of health benefits to all of its employees and their families. The company fully pays for the health benefits package, including extended health (prescription drugs, eye glasses, chiropractor, massage therapy and other health related services) as well as dental. There is a six-month waiting period for new employees to join the health benefit plan. Aboriginal employees with federal Indian Status health cards are given a $500 annual allowance towards health-related expenses not covered by their health card.

Other Benefits

A life insurance plan and a long-term disability insurance plan were added to the benefit package in 2005. The disability insurance premium is paid for by the employees through payroll deductions, so that in the event employees become disabled, income derived from this benefit would not be taxable. As it turned out, at least one family was able to benefit from the long-term disability coverage during the period of 2002 to 2010.

Other benefits include an allowance for safety boots and a tool belt with basic carpentry tools. This cost is repayable if the employee leaves ICR within three months of commencing employment. After three months' employment, the debt is forgiven and the equipment belonges to the employee.

In 2006, ICR set up a trial savings program whereby ICR contributes two dollars for every one dollar paid into the plan by the employee, up to a limit of a $500 contribution by ICR in one year. The program is modelled after the saving circle program administered by Supporting Employment and Economic Development (SEED) Winnipeg and supported by ACU. The saving circle program helps low-income individuals and families to save for necessities, including furniture, medical expenses, a computer, education, small business expenses or other household items. Although some employees take advantage of the incentive, most do not as they need their entire pay to cover daily and monthly expenses.

Housing

Suitable and affordable housing in Winnipeg was in short supply during the early 2000s. Prior to employment with ICR, many employees were homeless and staying in shelters, crashing with friends and relatives, or sleeping outdoors in parks or on the street. Those eligible for social subsidized housing were often on a waiting list.

Once employed by ICR, most employees are able to obtain suitable rental accommodation. ICR assists by providing employment letters for would-be landlords as well as security and/or first month rent deposits. Some single employees came together to rent an entire house and share the space. Others were housed in Manitoba Housing units in the North End. In a few cases, ICR employees were able to take advantage of the NEHP rent-to-own program. As an ICR shareholder, NEHP was sympathetic to ICR employees, who in many cases had been involved in the renovation of these same houses. In crisis situations, ICR financially assists employees to obtain rooms in inner city hotels catering to the homeless. There is no doubt that a full-time job and steady wages open up new and better housing opportunities for ICR employees.

Training

ICR is committed to training, both on the job and in the classroom. On-the-job training is provided by skilled crew supervisors, usually journeypersons, as well as by other skilled employees. Trainees observe how certain tasks are done and then do those tasks under supervision of their team leader. With time, they are assigned simple tasks on their own but never far away from a more skilled employee. This kind of training is very effective as most employees respond better to hands-on learning than learning in a classroom setting.

Employees are encouraged to pursue official apprentice training under the auspices of Apprenticeship Manitoba. Once registered in the program and sponsored by ICR, employees accumulate the necessary hours to fulfill the requirements for each level. Each of the four apprenticeship levels includes a ten-week classroom training course at the local community college. After successful completion of the four levels, apprentices are able to challenge the exam for journeyperson status.

As part of enabling employees to pursue this training, ICR pays the registration fees and provides the required textbooks. During the first eight years, approximately ten employees were enrolled in the apprenticeship program, and one completed all four levels and successfully passed the journeyperson exam. Another ICR employee with industry experience also successfully challenged the exam while employed by ICR. The other eight ICR employees completed and attained various levels towards their journeyperson status. This number may not seem like much considering ICR had 120 employees during its first eight years. However, only employees that have been with ICR for six months are eligible for the program, and considering the relatively high turnover rate, many employees do not attain the minimum employment period to qualify.

There is another factor imposed by Apprenticeship Manitoba for eligibility to the official apprenticeship training program: candidates need to have completed grade 10 English and mathematics. ICR tried various academic upgrading programs for employees who needed it in order to qualify. These programs included classroom instruction and one-on-one tutoring and were sensitive to different learning styles. None of the approaches was successful in getting these employees upgraded in order to be accepted into the apprenticeship program. However, some of these employees were with ICR for the entire eight years and became skilled through on-the-job training. Their wage rates have accordingly increased to reflect their improved skill levels and their long-term contribution to the company.

As well as providing the employee with a trade, with the potential for better wages, skills training increases opportunities for mobility and advancement in the construction industry. The general ongoing shortage of skilled labour in the sector means a long-term opportunity for those who learn a trade. Becoming more skilled, both with and without official accreditation, also increases employees' self-confidence. Being able to show others the direct results of their work, be it a residential renovation or a new commercial project, provides a sense of pride. Workers have been heard to say things like "I worked on this project," or more specifically, "I installed this window," or "I put up that wood panelling."

ICR also supports staff in other training and education programs. It sponsored one of its managers in the participatory management extension course offered at the University of Manitoba. Subsequently, a ten-session participatory management course based on the university course but tailored for ICR's employees has been offered to all supervisory and management staff. ICR also encouragesand supports supervisors to take a project management course at the local community college.

Employee Participation

Other aspects of employment that ICR considers parts of a quality job are opportunities for career advancement, participation in management and employee ownership. Opportunity for advancement within the company is encouraged and supported. Whenever possible, new leadership and middle management positions with increased responsibility and higher wages are filled from within the company. During the first eight years, several crew-members were promoted to lead hand positions, and one person graduating from the apprenticeship program was promoted to crew supervisor. Several crew supervisors have advanced into project management positions. The crew supervisor position requires journeyperson status and is usually filled from outside the company, as is the project manager position, which requires significant industry experience and knowledge.

Information regarding status of current projects, upcoming projects and financial performance is shared with all ICR employees. All employees are welcome to view monthly and annual financial statements, and verbal updates at monthly staff meetings include financial status of current projects and overall company profitability.

The monthly staff meetings and weekly supervisor meetings present opportunities for staff to learn about current issues and to make suggestions and provide ideas regarding any aspect of the company and its performance. Comments at the staff meetings tend to be limited to logistics — such as access to tools, delivery of materials, coffee breaks and so on — and their affects on productivity. However, safety is also a significant topic, and staff often offer safety suggestions related to specific situations. Social event planning always results in lively discussions. The weekly supervisor meetings tend to be more technical as supervisors discuss problems related to their projects and offer suggestions for solutions. These meetings are very useful as ideas and knowledge are shared among the participants.

Six months into the operation, three employee steering committees — employee rights and responsibilities, operations and social well-being — were struck through a democratic voting process. The employee rights and responsibilities committee did not last very long, but the other two committees continued, with the name of the social well-being committee changed to the social committee.

In the early years, rank-and-file employees were selected by their peers to attend and participate in ICR board of director meetings. After a trial period of a couple of years, this practice was dropped in 2005 due to lack of interest on the part of the employees, who saw it as a waste of their time. They stopped coming to meetings, finding excuses not to attend. In part, this was probably due to the meetings' subject matter, which often included finance, marketing and other administrative topics. I am sure that some employees were out of their comfort zone dealing with these topics, and consequently attending board meetings was an uncomfortable experience. In retrospect, it is clear that management could have done more training to make this experience interesting and comfortable for employees.

Potential for employee ownership was part of the quality job definition and was held out to employees as an option once the company had completed two consecutive profitable years and had accumulated positive equity. These criteria were not met, as the accumulated deficit was not eliminated until year eight. Although some staff liked the ownership concept, most rank-and-file staff were not enthusiastic about the prospect. Many employees were more concerned about their short-term income and their personal issues than with taking on the responsibility and risk associated with ownership.

Social Support

Working a full forty-hour week and showing up on time every morning are not easy for those coming out of institutional care, unemployment or any of the other situations related to a marginalized existence. This transition to full-time employment is very difficult for the employees and requires patience from ICR as well as a social support mechanism. Shortly after start-up, management realized that employees needed more support than ICR was able to provide both in terms of time and experience. The organization was fortunate to obtain the services of Larry Morrissette, a trained social worker, to assist with transitioning of its employees.

Larry is Aboriginal and grew up in Winnipeg's North End. He is thus familiar with the challenges faced by First Nations people in this community. Larry graduated from the Social Work Program at the University of Manitoba and subsequently taught there as well as in the Urban and Inner City Studies Program of the University of Winnipeg. He is a community activist and mentor in traditional Aboriginal culture and is a founder of Ogijiita Pimatiswin Kinamatwin (OPK), an organization to transition young Aboriginal gang members into productive construction-related work.

During his five years with ICR Larry provided individual counselling, mentoring and various social supports to ICR employees and their families. He dealt with issues of employee transition into full-time work, such as arriving on time on a daily basis. More importantly, he was a resource to ICR staff, dealing with issues related to addictions, family, the criminal justice system, housing and health. He was trusted by staff and able to refer them to community resources if and when necessary. In addition to his role as social worker he also organized social activities (e.g., sporting events, celebrations, family picnics and retreats) and traditional Aboriginal ceremonies (e.g., sweats and feasts). He organized memorials when ICR staff members died. Ceremonies recognizing Aboriginal employees for their positive life changes are led by Aboriginal elders and always include a feast.

One of the big differences between a private sector and a social enterprise workplace is the level of accommodation and supports provided to employees. Similar to other social enterprises, ICR makes accommodations for the realities of its workforce. Unlike the norms in the construction industry, where employees are fired for being late or a no show without calling in, ICR is more tolerant and provides employees with multiple chances to make the adjustment to full-time work. Those requiring specific assistance with addictions or other health issues are given a leave of absence in order to get the help they require, knowing that they have the opportunity to return once they are able and fit for work again. Harry (not his real name) was dealing with alcohol addiction, which limited his ability to work and affected the safety of his co-workers. He was encouraged to enter a treatment centre with the assurance that he could return to ICR once he was able to work again. Other employees take time off to deal with family matters knowing they can return, and some went to jail with the knowledge that they too could come back once they were released.

ICR also provides financial supports to employees in times of need. This includes funds for employees to travel to out of town to family funerals or for meeting rent payments when they have been off work due to illness or an accident.

Social Events

ICR provides not only employment but also an environment that includes social activities for all of its employees and their families. At all company gatherings and activities there is no-alcohol policy. During the early years, ICR's social worker arranged a number of sweats presided over by elders from the First Nations community. Sweats are an Aboriginal healing tool, a way to spiritual renewal and purification of body, mind, soul and spirit. The experience symbolizes a return to the womb (dark, moist, hot and safe) and the innocence of childhood. The experience can be a rebirth and a new start. A feast with a broad and plentiful selection of food and refreshments always follows the sweat. These sweats provide employees with an opportunity to change their lives and create a new beginning. Although both Aboriginal and non-Aboriginal employees, as well as both men and women are invited to attend, not all staff participate in the ceremony. There is an expectation that participants not drink alcohol or caffeinated coffee for several days prior to the sweat. There is also an expectation that one commits to making life changes. These expectations are taken very seriously within the Aboriginal community and therefore participation is not taken lightly.

ICR arranges and pays for quarterly social events such as pool or bowling outings. These two activities are favourites and attract more than half

ICR employees with hand-carved pipes they received at ceremony celebrating their life journey and accomplishments

of the staff. Another popular recreational sporting activity, which includes staff families, is the annual outing to watch Winnipeg's professional baseball team. In 2005, the Crocus Investment Fund let ICR use its corporate box at the ballpark for one game. This was a social highlight of the year for ICR staff. In 2007, I participated in a silent auction at a charitable event and won the use of a corporate box at the MTS Centre for a professional hockey game. ICR filled all the spaces in the box and again this event was one of that year's social highlight.

The most significant annual social event is a weekend retreat for all employees and their families. The retreat usually takes place in the spring, and ICR rents a leisure/conference centre in the Pine Falls area north of Winnipeg. The centre accommodates up to forty people, and usually between thirty and forty people participate in the retreat. The centre offers a general outdoor wilderness experience, which includes hiking, fishing and canoeing. ICR purchases all the necessary supplies for the weekend, and staff take turns preparing food and cleaning up. One of the best parts of the weekend is the fish fry. Pickerel caught in the river alongside the retreat centre are plentiful and taste great. Not everyone participates in the catching but all delight in eating the cooked fish. Some staff fish from shore and others from canoes, getting up early to claim what they consider to be the best fishing spots. There is always some chatter and kidding about licences and quotas as the Aboriginal staff do not need fishing licences and are not restricted to quotas, unlike non-Aboriginal staff. This does not affect the eating part as all

Larry Morrissette (ICR's social worker) and ICR employee fishing at weekend retreat

chow down on an equal basis. This event provides an opportunity for staff to socialize with each other and their respective families away from work and away from the city.

ICR employee at retreat with catch of the day

The annual seasonal celebration at Christmas is another favourite social event, and ICR and COS board members join staff in this seasonal celebration. Every year, Cheryl Lisoway, ICR's operations manager, takes great care in preparing gift packages for all of the employees. She approaches all of ICR's suppliers for contributions, and ICR purchases the remainder. Gift packages often include items of warm clothing, such winter coats, jackets, caps and toques, usually embossed with the ICR logo. Tools, both manual and power, are also a favourite gift. COS buys several larger gifts, such as DVD players and kitchen appliances, which are distributed at the event by pulling names out of a hat. In recent times, Cheryl also has begun to distribute gifts to spouses and other guests attending the event.

Annual seasonal celebration with ICR staff

A local caterer provides the food for the celebration, although in some years staff express a desire to prepare a potluck dinner themselves. In those years, ICR provides the turkeys and hams, which employees then cook at home and bring to the celebration. The meal usually includes perogies, vegetables, dressings and way too many desserts. Plain punch is served as quests arrive, and non-alcoholic wine is served with the meal. The annual talent show after the meal is very popular, with employees juggling, playing musical instruments, singing songs and telling stories. One year, two of the participants twirled flaming batons outside on Selkirk Avenue.

Scott Little, ICR employee, composed the following poem and recited it at the 2007 talent show:

> One sunny day, I decided to get a job.
> First day of work, they set me up with a builder named Bob.
> I felt like I was worked like a slave,
> On that day my supervisor was named Dave.
> All I had on my mind was when I'll get paid,
> And then I met a joker named Wade.
> All day I've thought of the rules I've bent,
> And then I compared myself to that leader named Brent.
> I've gotta tell you I'm an awesome carpenter, I aint lie'n,
> But there is a better one in the crew, his name is Brian.
> If there is one person on a site I would miss,
> It's that man of many talents, Chris.
> I am writing this poem to see what you'll give me,

I'm just trying to get my hustle on, just ask Jimmy.
I'd like to wish everyone a Christmas that is merry!
After this party, there's another hosted by Larry.
Some people may think I've been hell sent,
But I guess you all forgot about that crazy Nelson.
Lately I've worked with a guy named Andrew,
Who the heck let this guy run a crew?
Lately I've actually been able to hit a nail,
That's thanks to the criticism I've taken from Dale.
Tonight everyone gets a courtesy room at the Hilton,
Special thanks to taper Milton.
To the office I beg,
Please put me back on a crew with Craig.
I've been on drywall now since, I don't know when,
All day I have to put up with that big guy named Glen.
I met a nice guy you wouldn't believe,
He's from up north his name is Steve.
We all know how easy it is to get along with Harold,
As far as I can remember we don't employ a Jarrod.
I'm happy we haven't had to sing Christmas carols,
Because I wouldn't want to disappoint Cheryl.
This Christmas I asked Santa for an Atari,
But he immediately replied it was as ancient as Harvey.
I hope tonight you are filled with Joy and stuffed like a pita,
Can we all applause for such a great job being done by Anita.
So on this occasion to all a good night, but don't overdo it on the
      party,
Cause come Monday we'll have to answer to big bad wolf, Marty.
Your probably thinking I forgot about you didn't ya,
Don't worry we all love ya, Linda.

Dignity and Respect

ICR provides hope to its employees as well as to others in Winnipeg's inner city. They have hope that they'll be able to provide for their immediate family and assist their extended family; hope that comes from the sense of well-being associated with gainful employment; hope for a less stressful life; hope of leaving behind the violence associated with gang activities; hope for a new beginning for those coming out of incarceration; hope of setting an example for their children and the next generation; hope for dignity and respect.

All these kinds of hope are a reality for ICR's employees. Hunter and Travis were able to successfully leave behind a gang-related lifestyle. Clarence was able to obtain gainful employment for the first time after coming out

ICR staff in 2002

of prison.[8] Most employees express their gratitude for having been offered a second chance, an opportunity to turn their lives around. Jack and Tom received an opportunity to leave behind their dependence on social assistance, which in some cases has spanned several generations. Others are able to get their kids out of institutional care, now that they have a home to bring them to and an income to take care of them. For some with a mental health history, ICR provides the flexibility necessary to maintain a full-time job. Others, with intellectual challenges, are given an opportunity to be part of a conventional workplace, learn skills and earn money to supplement their support payments. Women interested in a non-traditional career in the trades are welcomed and supported. Individuals like Sylvester, with addiction issues, are able to beat their habits while employed in a supportive work environment. Regardless of the circumstances, ICR provides an opportunity to for people to change their lives in a positive way.

The employment provided by ICR is much more than a traditional job and a weekly paycheque. For many it is a new beginning or a transformation in their lives. It is a holistic experience affecting many parts of the employee's life.

Notes

1. Deane 2006.
2. <www.realestateforums.com/winnipegref/.../B2_DianneHimbeault.pdf>.
3. Comack and Silver 2006.
4. Silver 2012.
5. Silver 2012.
6. <http://conceptualmath.org/philo/minwage.html>.
7. Wilkinson and Pickett 2010.
8. Employee names in this section are not their real names.

Chapter 3

Employee Journeys

As an initiative to address poverty in the inner city, Inner City Renovation recruites unemployed residents, many of whom have difficult backgrounds. ICR's challenge as a socially conscious and responsible employer is to create an opportunity for personal change for its employees. This goal requires training, support and a lot of patience. As you will see from the personal journeys described in this chapter, the journey can be difficult for both the employer and the employee. However, these stories illustrate that regardless of the employee's difficult past and current situation, given an opportunity, positive life changes are possible.

Obviously, each ICR employee has their own unique life journey, but there are some similarities. Poverty, unemployment, addictions, mental health issues and a criminal record are common among the people who work at ICR. Many share the injustices related to institutional discrimination against Aboriginal people; some share experiences related to a gang lifestyle. As the following stories illustrate, employees have difficult and winding but very often successful journeys through ICR.[1]

Tom — Honing Skills and Stabilizing Life

Tom was born on one of Manitoba's First Nations and moved to Winnipeg in his early twenties. He was one of ICR's initial employees and was still at ICR at the time of writing. Working at ICR, he picked up drywalling skills, becoming one of the best tapers in the business and certainly the best taper at ICR. He is a committed and hard worker, often preferring to work right through his breaks. Tom loves hockey and plays regularly on a team in a North End industrial league. However, right from the start, Tom had a series of personal issues — including involvement in the criminal justice system, a violent street confrontation, accidents and family hardships — to contend with.

Shortly after ICR started up, he suffered a brutal unprovoked attack just outside his home. I outlined this event in a memo to the COS board:

> Every day we hear about horrific events in our community. Often they are anonymous to us and we thank our lucky stars that it didn't involve us personally. Once in a while however, it does move from the general to the personal. One such event, an unprovoked attack, occurred recently to an ICR crewmember, Tom. He sustained a fractured skull, cheekbone, jaw and left eye socket, as well as a number of other injuries. Luckily he lost consciousness after the first blow

and doesn't remember the rest of the assault. I didn't recognize him when I went to visit him in the hospital shortly after the attack. Four of the six youths involved in the attack have been apprehended and charged with attempted murder.

Tom will be off work for at least three months and although he will be eligible for EI benefits and crime victim benefits, these will take some time to take affect. He has a spouse and five children. ICR has set up a fund to support Tom and his family over the next few weeks. Your donations will be gratefully accepted on his behalf.

Hundreds of dollars were collected from staff and board members in response to this request.

Later that same year, in November 2002, Tom found himself in serious trouble with the justice system. He had been charged with breaching a non-molestation order, uttering threats and on several occasions failing to comply with a condition recognizance. At his court appearance, I promised to take responsibility for him in order to avoid his incarceration and signed a $1500 surety agreement. The conditions of the order were stringent. In addition to no contact and maintaining a minimum distance from his spouse, the order also included that he abstain from using and possessing alcohol, non-prescription drugs, firearms and weapons, as well as a 10 p.m. to 7 a.m., seven-day-a-week curfew restricting him to his home. In retrospect, it may have seemed foolish or naïve (or both) to place myself in such a precarious position with no assurance that Tom could or would be able to abide by the conditions. To his credit he did, and he avoided a jail sentence and I avoided losing my $1500.

Tom also suffered a couple serious accidents: one while riding his bike, and in another he was hit by a truck while walking to work. Somehow, he recovered from these injuries and was able to return to and maintain his employment. The most devastating events, however, were related to the loss of two close family members. His adult daughter died while she was on a holiday in Cuba, as a result of a fall from a hotel balcony, and then several years later, on February 25, 2010, he lost his wife, who was only forty.

During his tenure with ICR, like so many others of ICR's Aboriginal employees, Tom left Winnipeg and ICR for time to return to his First Nation, but always came back to Winnipeg and ICR. He remains one of ICR's key employees, providing valuable skills that he has honed over several years.

Tom is an example of an employee who has faced serious adversity, not only before his employment with ICR but also throughout his tenure. His story also illustrates the patience and support provided by ICR and its management staff. It is unlikely that Tom would have been able to cope with these challenges and maintained his job had he been employed in the private sector. Tom, ICR and the community are all better off. Tom is still employed, has developed his skills and is able to provide for his family. ICR has a skilled and committed employee, and the community has been spared support payments for Tom and his family.

Jack – Setting an Example for His Kids

Jack is also a First Nation member. He and his wife are raising seven children. Before starting at ICR, Jack and his family had been on social assistance. They lived in the North End on a street often referred to in the media as "murder alley." A local non-profit Aboriginal housing organization owned the house they lived in. From time to time, Jack fell behind in rent payments, which ultimately resulted in his family losing their home. Previously when he was short on rent money, ICR provided an advance in the form of a direct payment to the landlord. On the last occasion, Jack either forgot or was too proud to ask for another advance, and the sheriff's office evicted them. His children, ranging in age from four to sixteen, regularly got into trouble at school or skipped school altogether. The local neighbourhood gang was courting his young teenage sons, and his young daughter had her first child at fourteen and her second before her sixteenth birthday.

Jack works hard and takes pride in his work. He is well liked, loyal to the company and sets a good example for other employees. From time to time, Jack does not report for work. This is almost always related to family problems, especially concerning his children, who sometimes have gone missing for days at a time. By working, Jack tries to set a good example for his children. He is also a very proud individual who often resists assistance offered by ICR's social worker and management and by fellow workers. He has refused to take advantage of various social services available in the community to deal with his family issues.

Jack's story illustrates the reality of life for many residents in Winnipeg's North End and the adversity they have to deal with. It also shows the support and patience necessary to keep Jack gainfully employed so that he can be a role model for the next generation.

Clarence – Getting Kids Out of Institutional Care

Also born on a Manitoba First Nation, Clarence moved to Winnipeg early in his adulthood. He left behind a past that included chronic unemployment and domestic turmoil. Prior to coming to Winnipeg, Clarence had been in various relationships and fathered numerous children. When he first joined ICR, he was living alone without a spouse or children. Child and Family Services had taken his youngest two children into care. Clarence tried academic upgrading provided by ICR to get into the apprenticeship program, but he was unable to cope with the course. Primarily through on-the-job training he became a skilled carpenter and eventually secured the position of lead hand. Based on his employment with ICR and new ability to provide a home and care for his kids, he initiated proceedings to get his children back. In the meantime, he met a new partner and started a family with her. When the first child was still young and the second on its way, Child and Family Services stepped in and took their toddler into care and the second child as soon as it was born. This action was related to parenting issues and not his employment status. Clarence and his spouse took courses in anger management and parenting skills as part of an effort to get their kids back. At time of writing, a third child was on its way, and all of the children, both from their current relationship and from a previous one, had been returned to them.

Clarence was successful in stabilizing his life, starting a new relationship and getting his kids out of institutional care. His story also exemplifies the difficulty some employees have with obtaining the academic upgrading necessary for entrance into the apprenticeship program. However, if unsuccessful, ICR can provide sufficient on-the-job training to allow employees to develop their skills, advance and earn higher wages.

Archie – Moving On to Another Employer

Archie's stay with ICR was a bit of a roller coaster ride, as he twice left ICR and then came back to resume his employment. On one of these occasions, he moved his family to their First Nation in northern Manitoba, returning to Winnipeg after just a few months. Although he developed his skills, especially related to taping and painting, he was not always dependable. He was often late or sometimes failed to show up for work at all. On many occasions, I had to go to his home to wake him up. I even offered to buy him an alarm clock. His spotty attendance was often related to alcohol consumption, especially just after paydays. His ability to work was also hindered by a heart condition.

He attended most social events and contributed his musical talents at the seasonal party talent competitions. In 2009, after seven years with ICR, during which he practised and honed his painting and drywall skills, Clarence left ICR to work in the building maintenance department of a youth community service organization.

After one of ICR's interventions, which involved providing monetary assistance to his family, they expressed their appreciation by sending a note: "Thank you for being there for us in a time of need." Archie's training and support from ICR during his tenure allowed him to make the transition to another employer.

Elijah – Providing Timely Social Supports in Time of Crisis

Elijah was expressive and articulate. During his time with ICR, from 2002 to 2006, Elijah was an excellent spokesperson who promoted ICR at every opportunity. He appeared in interviews with the media and in promotional video clips. He was never at a loss for words and always spoke up at staff meetings. His interjections were at times critical of management and offensive to his co-workers, and sometimes his chatter got in the way of his work productivity.

Elijah had many issues that required a great deal of support while employed by ICR. On several occasions, he found himself homeless after altercations with his spouse. As was the case with some other ICR employees, Elijah had a restraining order to stay away from his spouse. They would mutually agree to get back together and then end up in an altercation. On one occasion his spouse locked him out of their home and put his personal belongings on the sidewalk. ICR put him up in a Main Street hotel until he was able to find a place to live.

Elijah had various health issues affecting his ability to work. Once, I visited Elijah in hospital while he was recovering from a heart episode. I also had an opportunity to visit him at Headingly jail while he was serving a sentence for violating a restraining order. Elijah had called me to bring his outstanding paycheque so that he could buy some smokes, which was still allowed in provincial jails at that point in time. This was my first inside look at a jail. The experience is imprinted in my memory, and I can still hear the clanking sound of the metal doors.

In 2006, after spending four years working at ICR, Elijah moved to British Columbia to take advantage of the construction labour market there. He is one of the few former ICR employees who maintained contact after leaving the company. Elijah was able to take the skills he learned at ICR and move on. His story also illustrates the extent of support ICR provided its employees, including visits to hospitals and prisons and providing temporary living accommodations.

Chester – First ICR Employee to Become Journey Carpenter

Chester had heard about ICR from some of our employees in the neighbourhood and decided to apply, joining ICR in 2002 shortly after the company started. He had recently arrived in Winnipeg after wandering from coast to coast to coast doing odd jobs but unable to settle down. His parents were very well educated, and Chester was also very bright but lacking in formal education. He could recite long poems from memory and speak intelligently about various issues and many topics, including world events and history.

Chester started out as a crewmember, applying some of the carpentry skills he had picked up along his journey. He had worked as casual labourer building fences and doing simple renovations. During his first year with ICR, he expressed an interest in pursuing the provincial apprenticeship program. Chester was the first employee to be sponsored by ICR in the program. He did extremely well, posting the highest marks in his class and completed the four-year program. The following year, in 2007, he successfully challenged the journeyperson's exam and passed with flying colours to obtain his carpentry journeyperson red seal ticket, which allows him to work as a carpenter anywhere in Canada.

Upon graduating as a journeyperson, Chester became a crew supervisor and took on some of ICR's most difficult and challenging projects, including the Neechewam and Ahsanook projects for Southern First Nations Network of Care. These were large-scale, complicated and high revenue (in excess of $1 million) renovation projects. As buildings in the Aboriginal community, they were also complex, with circular rooms. He was an excellent leader and teacher, providing training to other ICR apprentices. In 2009, he was nominated for the Manitoba Apprenticeship and Certification Board Journeyperson of the Year award and came in second in the province-wide competition encompassing all trades. In a matter of a few years, he had moved from being a novice to being a mentor. After years of wandering around the country, Chester finally found a permanent home in Winnipeg and more importantly he found himself. And his skills and commitment allowed ICR to take on more complicated commercial renovation projects.

Here is how Chester described his life leading up to employment with ICR:

> Life in Winnipeg's inner city is tough. Before I started working with ICR I felt useless. Oh, I had worked but each time I would get overwhelmed and then quit. Sometimes it was my drinking that caused me to miss work, and in those cases I was fired. One time I didn't have bus fare so I tried walking to my work but that day wasn't my lucky day. I just passed out. I hadn't eaten because I needed to pay our hydro bill or risk not having any power. We usually go to the food bank when we run out of food but I felt bad that when I had a job — but its hard keeping a job when you … that was before I started with ICR — ICR offered me more than a job. This was a company that cared.

Earl – Coping with Addiction

At my retirement celebration, Earl gave me a farewell card with the following message: "This is a sad time and an exciting time too. I am glad I was able to be part of the team. Sorry it took so long for me to grow up. I am thankful for your understanding and patience."

Earl joined ICR in 2002 as a journeyperson carpenter. Although very skilled in his work, he has spent a lifetime, including during his tenure with ICR, dealing with mental illness and addiction issues. From time to time he would go on a drinking binge and not show up at work for days. Sometimes he was verbally abusive and threatened to quit. He was on a lifelong roller-coaster ride with Alcoholics Anonymous, attending meetings regularly and then not attending for long periods of time. I gave him my home phone number and told him to call me anytime of day or night. ICR gave him a lot of slack to enable him to continue working. Despite these challenges, he was an asset to ICR and took on supervision responsibilities for large complicated commercial projects, including the construction of the north Main Street Assiniboine Credit Union branch. Although Earl was not the only employee dealing with addiction issues, he represented a particular challenge because of his leadership position in the company.

Chad – Coping with Tragedies and Starting a Stable Family Life

Chad joined ICR in 2008 as a trainee. He was born and raised in The Pas and is a member of Moose Lake First Nation. He has six siblings, some of whom he met for the first time while employed at ICR as four siblings were placed in care before he was born. At twenty-seven, he is a father of three children (one died as a toddler). He and his spouse live with two children, a seven-year-old from his spouse's previous relationship and their one-year-old. He rides his bike to work and works hard while there.

Chad left school after completing grade 9 but has since been assessed with reading and math skills at the grade 11 level, which is high enough to qualify him for the apprenticeship program. At the time of my departure, he was still on a waiting list to enroll in the program as ICR limits the number of employees in the program at any one time and gives priority to those who are employed by ICR longer.

The death of his father and followed by the death of his young daughter had a huge impact on him. His attendance at work was sporadic and he would seldom notify management when he was not going to be there. As a result his wages were frozen and he lost his priority for apprenticeship training. He has been able to put these tragic events behind him and concentrate on his own life with his new family and as a valuable and skilled employee at ICR.

Chad is a young employee trying to find his way and coping with family tragedies. He is also testing the boundaries of ICR's patience, which has caused some tension among ICR's management.

Vincent – Second Chance after Years in Prison

Vincent had spent a significant part of his life in prison before joining ICR in 2007, at which time he was in his late twenties and married and had two children. Vincent had little or no construction skills or experience, but he was willing to learn and was well liked by ICR's employees. He was employed by ICR for less than a year before leaving for construction work in Alberta. During a media interview he said, "Over the years I have taken a lot from society and now I am able to pay some of it back." This was in reference to his criminal past and the opportunity to work in a constructive environment for the betterment of the community.

Vincent exemplifies ICR's commitment to attract young people with gang affiliation and a criminal record and provide them with an opportunity to start a new life. Although Vincent's stay was short, it assisted him with the initial transition to a new life with gainful employment.

Bradley – Opportunity for Person with Intellectual Disabilities

In 2009, a support worker with SCE Lifeworks, an organization to support people with intellectual disabilities to work and participate in the community, contacted ICR. They were inquiring to see if ICR had an employment opportunity for one of their clients. We agreed to meet with the caseworker and their client, Bradley. Cheryl and I both took an immediate shine to Bradley. He was polite and engaging. He had never had a full-time job before and was eager to get the opportunity. We felt that there was a potential fit for him in our organization and hired him.

Bradley turned out to be dependable, punctual and a hard worker. He was big and strong and willing to take on various assignments. He ended up working on one of ICR's long-term commercial projects under Chester's guidance and supervision. This was a large project, with up to a dozen crewmembers. Bradley helped out by keeping a clean jobsite, transporting material and equipment and taking on demolition tasks as well as some repetitive renovation assignments. He learned to use power tools. He was well received and accepted by staff as one off their own. Bradley proved to be an asset and is still employed by ICR. His SCE Lifeworks support worker makes regular visits to see how he was doing. Bradley bikes to work most days, weather permitting. Bradley is a particularly good bowler and was a member on Team Manitoba in the National Special Olympics.

Homer – The Benefit of the Health Plan and Long-Term Disability

Homer is a journeyperson carpenter and a long-term employee with ICR. In 2005, at age fifty-five and unemployed, he approached the Path Employability Centre, associated with the North End Community Renewal Corporation. ICR has a continuing relationship with the Path Centre to screen and recommend potential employees. They recommended him and he started as a crew supervisor with ICR shortly thereafter. He was respected and well liked by all ICR employees. He taught carpentry skills and safety practices to many ICR employees.

Shortly after starting with ICR his physical health became an issue and he was promoted to the management team, as a project manager. While in this position, he participated on the company safety committee and was instrumental in developing the safety manual. Homer had been diagnosed with cancer, and as his health deteriorated, he was no longer able to work even at a desk position. Luckily for Homer, ICR had added long-term disability to the benefit plan, and Homer became the first employee to take advantage of the benefit. Health permitting, Homer still came to the office once or twice a week to volunteer and stay in touch with the employees. Homer had a wonderful sense of humour and often referred to ICR as "not a peanut butter operation." He passed away in February 2011.

Jill – Opportunity for Woman in Non-Traditional Work

Jill was one of about a dozen women crewmembers employed by ICR. She is Aboriginal with treaty status, married with a daughter and the sole financial provider in her family. Jill had heard about ICR from her friends in the community and applied for a position. She had been working with some of her family members in the construction sector and had developed considerable drywall and taping skills. She started with ICR in 2007 and specialized in drywall installation but also developed carpentry skills. Like so many other female employees in the male-dominated construction culture, she encountered difficulties being accepted by her male co-workers. ICR has a no-harassment policy and worked hard to get employees to abide by it. Jill left ICR in 2009 to move to Northwestern Ontario to be with her extended family.

Although running mixed crews has its challenges, ICR is committed to providing an equal opportunity work environment, one where women are welcomed and encouraged. ICR's female crewmembers prove that they are up to the task of working in a non-traditional trade.

Travis – Alternative to Gang Lifestyle

Travis came to ICR as part of a federal youth employment initiative, which subsidized his wages. A past gang member, his criminal record required that he have regular visits from his parole officer while working on ICR construction projects. Travis was employed by ICR for close to two years, from 2007 to 2009, and although hard working, he was not dependable. Travis often missed days at a time, without notification and no way to communicate with him. His attendance and lack of commitment to ICR were issues for dismissal; however, I personally advocated that we not give up on him.

When approached by the organizers of the Toronto Partners Solving Youth Homelessness Conference, in November 2008, I persuaded Travis to come with me and participate in the presentation. For his part, he told his life story to those gathered in the audience. He talked about his early years being raised by a single father who was an abusive alcoholic. As a young teenager, he was enticed into an Aboriginal gang. During his youth he was often homeless and fending for himself. Although not that different from other experiences shared by young people at this conference, his tragic story had a significant impact on the audience. As this was his first visit to Toronto, I took the opportunity to show him around, and we viewed Toronto from the top of the CN Tower and roamed through the Hockey Hall of Fame.

Travis left ICR in 2009. I had long suspected that he had maintained his ties to a gang while employed with ICR, which would explain his disappearances. Shortly after leaving ICR, he came back to see me and confirmed that he had been enticed back to gang life. He was worried about his future, especially possible re-incarceration, and indicated that he was leaving Manitoba to get away and start a new life elsewhere. Unfortunately, Travis's story is similar to those of many young Aboriginal men growing up in Winnipeg's North End.

Hunter – Alternative to Gang Lifestyle

Hunter came to ICR in 2002 from the Ogijiita Pimatiswin Kinamatwin (OPK) construction-training program, set up by Larry Morrissette to provide an opportunity for gang members to leave gang life behind and learn a trade. Hunter had been the leader of the Indian Posse, a well-known and established Aboriginal gang north of the railway tracks that divide Winnipeg. He was in his late twenties and married with two young children when he came to ICR. Hunter was a charismatic individual and accepted by the rest of the ICR employees. He tried hard to fit in, learning new skills and starting a new life with regular work hours. Unfortunately, as an ex gang leader with a criminal record, he was well known to the local police, and he was repeatedly apprehended and taken to the police station for questioning. The police assumed that he had knowledge about various crimes committed in Winnipeg's North End. This harassment affected his work performance as well as his commitment towards starting a new life.

On one occasion in 2003, shortly after he had started with ICR, he was detained and placed in jail. Upon his release, I met with him briefly and provided him with some clothing and food. He had decided to leave Manitoba and try to start a new life in another province. I never heard from him again. As with Travis and several others, Hunter's story exemplifies how ICR is able to provide a transition for those wanting to leave a gang existence.

Frankie – Coping with Chronic Diseases

Frankie was born and raised in Mathias Colomb Cree First Nation in Pukatawagon, Manitoba. While in his early twenties and still single, he moved to Winnipeg, participated in the Community Education Development Association (CEDA) carpentry training program and joined ICR at start-up in 2002. He was a quiet, reserved person and well liked by his co-workers. He worked diligently, learning additional carpentry skills along the way.

He always showed up for work on time and never missed a day. That is why it was so unusual when on a cold wintery morning in early 2003 he did not report for work. While waiting for his bus, he collapsed and he was pronounced dead before arriving by ambulance at the nearby hospital. It is suspected that Frankie died from complications related to diabetes.

ICR employees attended his community memorial service and participated in a special Aboriginal ceremony arranged by ICR's social worker to mark his passing. At the ceremony, in keeping with Aboriginal custom, a blanket with Frankie's personal belongings was laid out and each ICR staff member was invited to take an item from the blanket in his memory. I chose and still have his tool belt.

Changing Lives

As these stories dramatically show, the people who work at ICR, the people who are the *raison d'être* of ICR, have traumatic and challenging, yet interesting and hopeful lives. Trying to be the vehicle to help others change their lives is also challenging. The traumas and troubles they bring, along with with their desire to make a significant change, require much of everyone involved, from co-workers to managers. The typical capitalist firm, motivated primarily to profit, would most surely not see the need to be both an ally and an employer with workers such as these. Their stories also show that with the challenges come great enjoyment, inspiration and exhilaration for the people who function as allies for people transitioning to a better life.

ICR's social goals are ambitious, and progress is taking much longer than first anticipated. Although there is continual movement related to the social justice goals, it is clear that the alleviation of systemic poverty is a long-term project that will span generations. With time, ICR's expectations had to be altered: making large, long-lasting impacts is too ambitious. Achieving small changes in the current generation is more realistic, and along with that comes the realization that the experience of small changes will lead to more significant changes in subsequent generations.

Responsibility in managing a social enterprise like ICR, with its focus on employment goals, can feel overwhelming. Most conventional employers do not feel responsibile for the employees and their families. I often gave or loaned cash to employees to buy groceries, diapers or other life necessities when their money had run out before payday. This additional sense of responsibility related to the employees can feel like a burden at times, but in a social enterprise it is difficult to disassociate the enterprise from employees' personal challenges.

Working predominantly with Aboriginal employees, which is the case with ICR, presents a challenge in itself. Most conventional corporations do not make adaptations for Aboriginal culture and practice, and I was a relative novice in these matters when I joined the organization. During my years at ICR, I was introduced to and participated in several Aboriginal ceremonies and cultural events. I endured the heat along with ICR's employees in sweat ceremonies and ate heartily afterwards during the feasts. At a pipe ceremony marking major life transitions for two of ICR's employees, I was presented with a buffalo skull by the elder presiding over the ceremony. I learned afterwards that the buffalo represents a nurturing quality by providing food, shelter and protection in Aboriginal culture. I felt very honoured to receive this gift.

ICR, however, went further in attempts to adapt to Aboriginal culture and achieve its social justice (employment) goals by employing a "social worker." Working with Aboriginal employees required the assistance of an Aboriginal person. Larry Morrissette, a man with an extensive background in helping and in Aboriginal culture, not only assisted ICR employees with their personal issues but was also a mentor to ICR and its management.

Making social justice a real enterprise goal also means coping with tragedies and grief. This is an unavoidable aspect of managing a social enterprise, especially in a setting like Winnipeg's North End. Several of ICR's employees and numerous immediate family members died as a result of accidents, illnesses or violence. In each case, ICR employees attended the funeral or family memorial. There were also numerous visits to hospitalized employees. Some were suffering from the affects of diabetes, some from violence and others from injuries related to the workplace. In a social enterprise, with the emphasis on people, tragic events tend to take on a larger and more emotional significance than in conventional corporations.

Learning to cope with disappointment was also a challenge. One of the biggest disappointments was losing some of the young employees who were enticed back to gang culture. As a manager, I often took it as a personal failure, wondering if somehow I could have done more and prevented them from falling back into that lifestyle. There is also the disappointment associated with having to turn away many worthwhile applicants. ICR was only able to hire a small fraction of the many applicants.

At times it was frustrating as individual employees suffered relapses or encountered new challenges. Even with supports in place, some employees were unable to make the transition towards regular full-time employment. I personally feel that we failed these individuals, that the supports and collective patience were insufficient. ICR management learned that individual and social change are not linear. They include ups and downs, triumphs and setbacks, one step forward, two steps back; they take time.

Social enterprises and their employees require strong leadership. People tend to respond positively to a leader they trust and can relate to. Whenever and wherever possible, I pitched in and worked along side ICR's employees. This setting-by-example leadership style was put to good use and tested during my time at ICR.

As illustrated in these employee journeys, employment at ICR, along with its income, benefits, social supports and training, was for many a life changing experience. For ICR, these journeys present a major challenge. Dealing with employee related issues while delivering a quality and competitive service is indeed difficult. The rewards of seeing people flourish make it all worthwhile.

Managing a social enterprise and working towards its social justice goals requires patience, lots of patience. The years I spent at ICR taught me that patience and to appreciate incremental steps forward. If the story of ICR set out in Chapter 1 shows the need to have business goals, skills and practices in a social enterprise, the stories in this chapter and the years I spent at ICR taught me that managers and leaders in a social enterprise must be truly committed to social justice goals if the enterprise is to succeed.

Note

1.   Employee names in this chapter are not their real names.

Chapter 4

From Corporate Honcho to Social Justice Worker

I was involved with Inner City Renovation from its very beginning. But, thirty years ago, there was not much indication that I would end up in an organization like ICR. Over those thirty years, I went from a corporate executive position on Bay Street in Toronto to managing a social enterprise in Winnipeg's North End. I went from wearing business suits, flying in corporate jets and travelling around the world to working in one of the most challenging inner city communities in all of Canada. While this journey may seem strange and contradictory, it illustrates the dual track of social enterprise: the need for a commitment to social justice and business experience, both of which were critical to the success of a social enterprise like ICR.

Corporate Career Crisis

My corporate career reached a crisis point in 1985, while I was employed in a division of Noranda Inc. I had a major confrontation with the president of the company during which I was told that I should adopt the company's corporate values in lieu of my own personal values. A number of events had transpired over the preceding years leading up to this point.

As manager of international sales, I had taken issue with sexist ads appearing in a *Timber Trade Journal* in the United Kingdom, an industry journal patronized by Noranda. I had notified the magazine's management that our company would withdraw its advertising if the journal continued to include blatantly sexist ads. The journal's management, somewhat surprised by my criticism, contacted our U.K. director. Although I was his boss, the U.K. director bypassed me and communicated with our company president back in Toronto. I was subsequently told that I had to withdraw my ultimatum and apologize. I refused, and our president took it upon himself to apologize on my and the company's behalf. This was the start of a deteriorating relationship.

I joined Noranda in 1980 after graduation with an MBA degree from York University in Toronto. I started out in the marketing department of Noranda's forest product division and was soon promoted to the marketing manager position. This was followed by a promotion to head up the international sales department with regional corporate offices in the U.K. and Japan as well as independent sales agents throughout continental Europe. I loved the position, especially the travel that took me around the world. Hedging currencies to protect sales made in foreign currencies for shipment and payment at a future date was a challenging part of the work. Managing long-term cargo vessels under lease to Noranda was another challenging aspect even though I had a subordinate solely responsible for shipping to foreign markets.

I was soon promoted again to head up the corporate planning group. I found myself conducting feasibility studies for new plant startups in places like Bemidji, Minnesota, and Inverness, Scotland. At the same time, the company was shutting down an existing plant producing the same product in Chatham, New Brunswick, that was no longer meeting profitability expectations, partially due to distance from major markets such as the U.S. Midwest and the U.K. The impact of the plant shutdown in a one-company town was devastating to the community. This reality was troubling to me personally, and I said so at our management meetings. Along with my earlier confrontation regarding sexist advertising, this was not taken well by management, who started to view me as out of synch with corporate values.

By 1984, the rift between my personal and corporate values reached a crisis point. My superiors started to pressure me to fall in line. It started with some joking, such as: you are not really serious about your views, are you? This escalated to threats: you will do this or else. When these tactics were not persuading me to fall in line, I was isolated in my corner office as a *persona non grata*. None of my former staff or colleagues would communicate with me for fear of consequences to their careers. This continued for nearly six months. I would go in every day and sit in my office ready for work, but there was no work for me as all of my responsibilities had been reallocated. Then one day, representatives from a human resource management firm specializing in firing executives came to my office to tell me that I was no longer employed. Having watched me pack up my things, they escorted me out of the building. The management consultants were directed to negotiate a severance settlement package and provide assistance in my finding a new position. I went home that day feeling very relieved, like the weight of the world had been lifted off my shoulders. My spouse and I celebrated with a bottle of champagne to mark the occasion.

Transition

While still in my corporate position, I had met Don Altman in a chance encounter at Toronto City Hall. Upon learning about my business background, he invited me to participate in a think-tank that was discussing alternative economic models, including cooperatives and employee ownership. The group was composed of academics Jack Quarter and Jack Craig, lawyers Brian Iler and Laird Hunter, and co-op/credit union activists Mark Goldblatt, Judy Skinner and Don Altman.

I felt at home in this environment and was excited when presented with an opportunity to assist the employees of Canadian Porcelain in Hamilton, Ontario, to purchase their plant. Canadian Porcelain had been shut down and placed in receivership. It was the last Canadian company producing porcelain insulators for electrical transmission lines. The company had been profitable at the time of closure, but the owners felt that they could make more profit by investing their capital elsewhere. The closure placed more than a hundred employees out of work. Bill Thompson, shop steward of the local union, led the employee buyout attempt. I was hired to work with the employee buyout group and produce a business plan to secure financing and ultimately to convince the receiver that an employee buyout was a viable option. The business plan was produced in less than two weeks and was successful in obtaining financing commitments from a consortium of local credit unions. The receiver paid little or no attention to the business plan, as they were simply not interested in an employee buyout. Instead, they accepted a bid from Canadian Porcelain's main competitor in the United States.

At an early point in the buyout attempt, the CBC television program *Venture* became interested in the story and started documenting and filming the process. They attended buyout committee meetings, union meetings and meetings with the receivers, all the while filming the process. After the buyout was turned down, they documented a demonstration by the workers at the Royal Bank head office in downtown Toronto. The workers were angry with the Royal Bank, which, while acting as the receiver, refused to consider their buyout offer. Out-of-work Canadian Porcelain employees were bussed to downtown Toronto to picket outside the Royal Bank head office. The workers were convinced that the only reason for the purchase by the U.S. competitor was to get the customer order file and avoid another company from competing with them in the Canadian market. They predicted that the Canadian plant would be shut down within a year after the purchase.

In the early 1980s, the Foreign Investment Review Agency (FIRA) was still active in reviewing all foreign takeovers of Canadian companies. Sinclair Stevens was the minister in charge of the agency at the time. The employee buyout group sent a delegation to Ottawa to meet with the minister in an effort to prevent the foreign takeover. CBC's *Venture* tried to document this meeting as well but was refused permission by the minister's staff. Shortly after the meeting with the minister, FIRA approved the sale to the U.S. competitor. As it turns out, this was the last case reviewed by the foreign investment review agency for it was shut down shortly thereafter and subsequently replaced with Investment Canada. The workers' fear that the plant was being bought for the order file and to keep the plant from falling into a competitor's hands actually occurred. The Canadian plant in Hamilton was shut down within a year after the purchase, and as predicted by the workers, the order file was transferred to the parent company's facilities in the U.S.

Although the buyout attempt was unsuccessful, the experience for me had been exhilarating and propelled me into a new career of consulting in the social economy. It was as if I had found a home, a place were my personal values meshed with my work. By this time, the think-tank group had already founded the Worker Ownership Development Foundation (WODF), a national organization with charitable status to provide education on employee ownership and worker cooperatives. As a separate initiative to do advocacy work, a worker cooperative consulting group called Co-op Work was set up by Wally Brandt, Bob Allan and myself. Unlike Bob and Wally, who were drawn to social justice work related to their Jesuit past, I was drawn by my desire for a more egalitarian economic system.

Co-op Work

Co-op Work provided assistance to both existing worker co-ops and groups interested in setting up a worker cooperative. One of Co-op Work's first projects was to help The Big Carrot, a small worker cooperative that operated a retail health food store in Toronto. It was doing very well and had outgrown its retail space. I introduced Mary Lou Morgan, the leader and founder of The Big Carrot, to David Walsh, a Toronto businessperson and philanthropist interested in combining development ventures with social good. The meeting led to The Big Carrot becoming the anchor store in Carrot Common, a retail/office complex on the Danforth across from the original Big Carrot store. Co-op Work provided the business plan for The Big Carrot to raise the capital for its expansion. The plan was successful in raising $250,000 in preferred (non voting) shares. Upon completion of Carrot Common complex, the Worker Ownership Development Foundation (WODF), Co-op Work and Bread & Roses Credit Union as well some other community organizations moved into office space on the second floor.

Around this same time, Co-op Work was also hired as consultants on the Burwash project, located just outside of Sudbury, Ontario. Burwash was a closed-down federal correctional facility that had been in mothballs for years and was slowly deteriorating. It was built in 1914 and closed in 1973. The facility included a hospital, post office, small shops, dairy barns, slaughterhouse, sawmill, elementary school, laundry facilities, power generation and a greenhouse, all on 35,000 acres of beautiful farmland.

The Sudbury Citizens Coalition, led by Joan Kuyek, wanted to turn the facility into something useful to the community before it deteriorated beyond repair. Part of their plan was to set up a number of worker co-ops to use different parts of the facility. The coalition hired Peat Marwick and Partners as the primary consultants for the project and directed them to sub-contract Co-op Work for the development of worker co-ops. I am not sure if the main consultants took the worker co-op component or Co-op Work seriously.

The Peat Marwick consultants were charging their senior consulting staff out at ten times the normal charge-out rate for Co-op Work consultants. In order to be taken more seriously, Co-op Work increased its charge-out rate to approximately half of their rate. The assignment identified a number of feasible worker co-op enterprises for the site. The federal government, however, was indecisive about its plans for the future of the site and did not pursue the Sudbury's Citizen Coalition proposal. The site was bulldozed and demolished in 1994, twenty-one years after it was closed down. Working in partnership with a large international consulting firm was a significant learning opportunity for me personally as well as for Co-op Work. The learning experience included the research methodology, the report writing and the fees charged. The biggest learning, however, was that the two volume report by established mainstream consultants did nothing to sway the government in supporting the proposal by the Sudbury Citizens Coalition.

Co-op Work provided assistance to worker co-ops across Canada with projects from St. John's, Newfoundland/Labrador, to Vancouver, British Columbia. It assisted in the development of a worker co-op providing a cleaning service in St. John's and assisted Community Resources Systems (CRS), a worker co-op engaged in the distribution of health food in Vancouver and the lower mainland.

The international development arm of the Canadian Co-operative Association hired Co-op Work to support worker co-ops in Costa Rica. Although Co-op Work was an important resource and provided valuable assistance for worker co-ops, there was an insufficient demand for its services as well as a lack of funds to support it. Even though worker co-ops were flourishing in Quebec, in part due to the support of the provincial government there, worker co-ops were not catching on in other parts of Canada.

In 1986, Co-op Work was dissolved, and I started a new consulting business in partnership with Karen Knopf. We called the partnership Coady Consulting, after Moses Coady, the Jesuit who was instrumental in developing co-ops and credit unions in Antigonish, Nova Scotia. We set out to provide management consulting services to non-profit community organizations, foundations, credit unions and labour unions. Clients included International Ladies Garment Workers Union (ILGWU), Pink Triangle Press and Universities and Colleges Credit Union (currently Alterna Savings and Credit Union Ltd.).

It was during this time that I became involved with developing A-Way Express, a courier enterprise to create employment for people with mental health issues. Coady Consulting was hired by Houselink Community Homes and Progress Place to come up with a viable concept for an enterprise to provide employment for mental health survivors. Together with the two partner organizations and the survivors, we came up with an enterprise concept. The business plan called for the use of the public transit system as the transportation mode for courier deliveries. This was well suited to the employees as a safe, fast and easy method to get around. After more than a year of planning, community developers Jacques Tremblay and Cynthia Carlton provided the leadership to its start-up in June 1987. Twenty-five years later, A-Way Express is still operating as a courier business in Toronto. With around 70 employees, it is a model for employment creation in the mental health field. A-Way has enabled many survivors to reclaim their place in the community and take back their lives.

My Formative Years

This newfound happiness with my career was in some way in keeping with my roots. I was born in Rotterdam, Holland, on May 7, 1945, the day that Rotterdam was liberated by the Canadian forces at the end of the Second World War. My parents were relatively poor working-class people. I spent the first nine years of my life in Holland. Our family immigrated to Canada in March 1955, following my older brother, who had done so a year earlier. Upon arriving in Toronto, where my parents settled, I started elementary school without knowing any English. I was not alone in this predicament as boatloads of Europeans were arriving regularly to start a new life in Canada. My childhood in Toronto was quite uneventful except for being labelled and taunted at school as a "DP" (slang for "displaced person"). This prompted me to learn English faster and not to speak Dutch in public. Like most other Canadian boys at that age, I started to play hockey, a sport that I continued to play competitively into my mid thirties.

As I was growing up in Toronto, I took on a number of part-time jobs for spending money and more importantly to pay for my education. As a young teenager, I spend several years selling sundries at Maple Leaf Gardens. It gave me an opportunity to see NHL hockey games for free while earning a few dollars. Summer jobs during high school years included working at Presswoods, a hog slaughtering and packaging facility in the Toronto stockyards. Throughout my high school years as well as my years during my undergraduate program at university, I worked at the Old Mill Restaurant on the banks of the Humber River. For the first few years, I worked as a bus boy and later as a waiter and bartender. This job took up most of my leisure time; consequently, my memory of those years is related to work and school.

During my summers while at university, I worked as a laboratory technician in the pulp and paper section at the Ontario Research Foundation and co-authored a research paper on pulping black spruce. I also spent a summer working at Engineered Timber Products, a structural glue-laminated beam fabricator. As a summer intern, I took on many different assignments including preparing simple designs and responding to tenders in an effort to obtain contracts. The variety of work during my adolescence, including factory labour, sales, waiting on tables, laboratory research and structural timber design, exposed me to various types of work. It was also a precursor to my future interests in entirely different areas.

My parents were hard working people and set an example for a disciplined approach to work and life in general. They were also caring people who shared what they had with others who had less than them. These lessons influenced me in later years.

As a son of immigrant working-class parents, I was encouraged to pursue higher education so that I could do better than them. Neither of my parents had gone beyond elementary school. Upon graduation from high school, I was accepted at the Faculty of Engineering at the University of Toronto. After my first year, I transferred to the Faculty of Forestry and graduated with a BScF, with a specialty in wood science and timber engineering.

After graduation, I was presented with an opportunity to be the technical counsellor in eastern Canada for the Plywood Manufacturers of British Columbia, a trade association representing the plywood producers in B.C. This position allowed me to meet with engineers and architects, to give guest lectures at universities across eastern Canada and to work on the Metric Commission. The Metric Commission was a federal agency charged with converting the imperial measurement system to metric in Canada. I was on a committee dealing with conversion in the forest products sector. A few years later, in 1975, I pursued a position in the federal public sector as an industry liaison officer with the Eastern Forest Products Laboratory of Environment Canada in Ottawa. This was an Ontario-based position liaising between research and industry. My responsibility was to identify research projects helpful to the forest products industry and at the same time relay completed research to industry for implementation.

It was during this time, that I realized that my education was lacking in business management skills and I enrolled in the MBA program at York University on a part-time basis. Having already started a family, balancing my time between home, studies and work was quite difficult. My studies in the MBA program were interrupted for three years when I accepted an opportunity to live and work in London, England, in a public relations position on behalf of the Council of Forest Industries of British Columbia (COFI). This position provided access to the business establishment in the U.K. I attended functions at various Canadian embassies in Europe and a variety of industry events. I felt comfortable in these surroundings even though they were a long way from my family roots.

It was also during this time in the U.K. that I was introduced to feminism. I had reconnected with a high school friend who introduced me to feminist philosophy. I read a number of feminist books popular at the time and that have since become classics. This exposure to feminism played an important role in my subsequent years at Noranda, where my personal values were at odds with corporate values. When my three-year contract with COFI in the U.K. was over in the summer of 1979, I returned to Canada to complete my MBA program on a full-time basis.

Policy Advisor in Ontario Provincial NDP Government

The travel, exposure to other cultures, meetings with international business leaders were all key elements that influenced me in later years as I tried to find my way in the business world. During my years at Inner City Renovation in Winnipeg, my previous exposure to Aboriginal culture and issues was a significant asset. When the New Democratic Party (NDP) won the provincial election in Ontario on October 1, 1990, the minister responsible for natural resources and native affairs approached me to join his political staff as his senior policy advisor for forestry issues. After some deliberation, I agreed and dissolved the Coady consulting partnership to pursue this new opportunity. The NDP's decision to combine natural resources and native affairs under one minister was part of a government effort to lay the groundwork for self-government in First Nations. As the minister's senior policy advisor on forestry issues, I was instrumental in developing a sustainable forest policy that included protecting old growth forests and making sure that forests were sufficiently regenerated. I also brought together the various stakeholders in the Temagami area, where Bob Rae had been arrested during a protest rally before he became premier of Ontario. The Temagami Stewardship Council, which included Chief Potts of the Temagami First Nation, was given management responsibility of a large tract of land in this region. I spent nearly four years with Minister Wildman and his political staff, moving with him to Energy, Environment and Native Affairs after a mid-term cabinet shuffle. This exposure to government and its inner workings was a real asset when setting up ICR.

A New Start in Winnipeg

Before the NDP term in office ended in the next provincial election, I moved to Winnipeg with my partner, who had been hired in Sociology Department at the University of Manitoba. We arrived in Winnipeg in the summer of 1993 and settled in Osborne Village, in the centre of Winnipeg.

After taking some time to recover from four demanding years as a political staffer, I pursued an opportunity with the newly developed Crocus Investment Fund, an investment fund sponsored by the Manitoba Federation of Labour. It was a tool to provide investment capital in Manitoba, which gave both provincial and federal tax credits for investors. Crocus was looking for a person to start-up their investment department, and in January1994, I joined as vice-president of Investment. Although I had no prior venture capital experience, my background with financing start-ups in the social economy sector coupled with my corporate business experience was considered ideal for the position. After a couple of years and several successful investments, it became clear that there was a lack of opportunity to invest in socially conscious enterprises. That coupled with the rate at which money was being invested in the fund necessitated a change in the investment philosophy and ultimately in my leadership in that position. I subsequently transferred to manage the client services department, which dealt with all aspects of the fund's relationship with investors, who were primarily individual Manitobans investing for their retirement. This was a relatively short-lived position as I was not happy in this administrative role.

When Garry Loewen, an employee with the Mennonite Central Committee (MCC), was in the process of setting up the North End Community Renewal Corporation (NECRC) in the North End of Winnipeg, he approached the Crocus Investment Fund for assistance. The fund agreed to second me to NECRC as its director of business development in the North End of Winnipeg, a position I readily accepted.

This was my first real exposure to Winnipeg's North End. The office was located on Selkirk Avenue in a building purchased by MCC, not far from Oretski, a renowned local department store, which had long been boarded up. In fact, we were surrounded by boarded-up commercial properties, including a Woolworths store, several banks, the Palace Theatre and Clifford's, a former clothing store. Of all commercial properties on Selkirk Avenue between Main Street and McGregor Avenue (about one kilometre), more than 50 percent were closed. This figure was even higher on the block between Parr and Andrew Streets, where more than 70 percent of the buildings were boarded up. This presented a significant challenge to the community and NECRC. During the two years of my secondment, I was able to attract several major organizations to the neighbourhood, including the Urban Circle Training Centre, which ended up purchasing and renovating the old Woolworths, and the University of Manitoba, which demolished the old Oretski and Clifford properties to make room for a new building for the School of Social Work.

It was also during this tenure with NECRC that I saw first hand the impacts of poverty on the community, the role of Aboriginal gangs, the lack of adequate housing and employment opportunities, and general safety issues. All of this was useful background for the subsequent development of COS, a charity committed to the alleviation of poverty in Winnipeg's inner city.

Community Ownership Solutions/Inner City Renovation

Upon completion of my secondment with NECRC, I returned to the Crocus Investment Fund to participate in the development of a charity to assist in inner city poverty alleviation. Community Ownership Solutions was incorporated in 1999, and I was hired as its general manager. This led to the development of social enterprises and the start-up of Inner City Renovation Inc. After several years as an ICR board member and of supporting the enterprise, I was asked by the COS board to take over the general manager position in 2006. I continued in this position till my departure in July 2010.

Social Enterprise and Social Justice Values

The social justice values I acquired during my life journey were critical to my role in managing Inner City Renovation. The values related to helping others instilled by my parents and my exposure to feminism in the seventies were instrumental to developing my social justice values. The hard work associated with growing up in an immigrant family prepared me for the hard work associated with starting and managing a social enterprise. The experience associated with the plant shutdown in Chatham, New Brunswick, while still in my late thirties, was instrumental in my developing commitment to social justice. In fact this event was the turning point in my life.

My business management experience, acquired over the years in various corporate positions, provided me with not only management tools but also insight into management practices. I developed a leadership quality so important in managing a social enterprise.

My two terms with government, as a civil servant in the federal government and political policy advisor in the Ontario provincial government, gave me insights into government practices and accessing assistance. Social enterprises, especially in their start-up phase, usually require government assistance, and ICR was no exception. These government roles in addition to my terms in venture capital and management consulting were critical experience related to the financing of a social enterprise.

My work with the employee buyout of Canadian Porcelain in Hamilton provided me with valuable experience in community and public activism. Shortly thereafter my assistance to local indigenous groups in Costa Rica who were setting up worker co-ops prepared me for dealing with the poverty in Winnipeg's North End.

The combination of social values, ingrained by my experiences, and business skills, developed while working in the corporate sector, were instrumental in my ability to manage a social enterprise. These two aspects do not need to be in contradiction with each other; in fact they can be complementary. It is as if my life journey had been preparing me for my role in the development of a social enterprise.

Working in Winnipeg's North End, I witnessed the challenges related to poverty and systemic discrimination. For the first time in my life, I entered a prison, once to visit an ICR employee who had been incarcerated at Headingly prison, and on another occasion to participate in a job fair at Stony Mountain penitentiary. I also experienced the judicial system by signing a $1,500 surety agreement with very stringent conditions in order to keep one of ICR's employees out of jail. I learned to deal with North End landlords providing substandard housing and evicting tenants when they were late in making rent payments. These experiences presented new horizons for me personally. They also illustrate the challenges inherent in managing a social enterprise with inner city residents facing multiple barriers.

Part 3

SOCIAL AND POLITICAL ISSUES

Chapter 5

Renewing Communities

In addition to creating employment in inner city neighbourhoods, ICR is also committed to community renewal, both in terms of infrastructure, including houses and commercial buildings, and in terms of community safety and general well-being. ICR does infrastructure renewal projects throughout Winnipeg's inner city, but the most of the work is concentrated in the North End.

Residential Renewal in Winnipeg's Inner City

ICR works at community renewal largely through improving the housing stock in the inner city. It does this both by renovating houses and by building new houses. Safe, energy efficient, well-built houses are then offered to inner city residents.

The feasibility study for ICR, completed before its start-up, identified a significant need for renovation services related to the deterioration of residential properties in Winnipeg's inner city. In the late 1990s, there were many derelict, boarded-up houses, which were not only an eyesore in the community but a prime target for arsonists. The city had responded to this problem by setting up the Arson Task Force, which dealt with the immediate problem by demolishing some dilapidated houses, removing temptations such as overfilled garbage containers and catching some arsonists, but it did not deal with the root of the problem, which is poverty.

The ICR feasibility study identified that in addition to these boarded-up deserted properties, there were many occupied houses in need of major repair. It also found that there was a shortage of affordable and adequate housing in the community. These factors had prompted the creation of the North End Housing Project (NEHP), a non-profit community organization, to renovate derelict properties and bring them back on the market as rent-to-own properties for local residents. Shortly after NEHP was established, the organization became a founding shareholder in ICR. NEHP was attracted to ICR's holistic approach to provide employment and training to local residents, while at the same time renovating dilapidated houses to provide new housing for local residents. As part of its relationship with NEHP, ICR renovated well over a hundred houses in Winnipeg's North End. At the same time, it also renovated houses for Spence Neighbourhood Association and West Broadway Community Development Corporation, two local non-profit community organizations involved with housing in their respective neighbourhoods.

As part of the renovation process on all of these properties, houses were completely gutted and rebuilt, including new electrical, plumbing and mechanical systems. Particular attention was given to making them energy efficient, thereby reducing future operating costs. The market value of these homes, due to their location in the inner city, was considerably less than the capital cost for acquisition and renovation, which exceeded $100,000, while the selling price was considerably less. The Winnipeg Housing and Homelessness Initiative provided grants to cover the gap, which was often as much as $50,000.

To increase the impact of the program, housing renovations were clustered: three or four renovated houses on one block made more of an impact than scattered ones throughout a larger neighbourhood. Most of the clustering in the North End occurred on streets adjacent to Selkirk Avenue, between McGregor Avenue and Main Street. As more and more houses were renovated, the property values in this neighbourhood started to increase, reversing years of declining property values.[1] In fact, the success of the program and resulting increasing property values started to have a prohibitive effect on the financial viability of the renovation program. Although this is counter intuitive, it is because the increase in purchase price of the dilapidated houses was greater than the increase in market value of the renovated home. This was mainly a result of increases in the value of the land not the structure itself. At the same time the city, which often sold dilapidated houses to the community housing organizations for one dollar, was now starting to capitalize on the increased land values and selling dilapidated properties at market value based on the land.

New Housing

During its relationship with NEHP, ICR started building new residential houses on vacant lots in the city's core as part of the city's infill housing program. As the acquisition and construction costs for renovating existing houses approached or exceeded that of building new houses, there was a push towards building new rather renovating old houses.

At first ICR built a few new houses for NEHP, but it wasn't until a year or two into its relationship with the Housing Opportunity Partnership (HOP) that it built about ten infill houses over a two-year period. HOP is a not-for-profit organization set up by the WinnipegRealtors group and is committed to providing social housing and participating in the rejuvenation of the West End of the city core. In 2006, ICR entered into a relationship with HOP that lasted until 2010, when the city's infill program decided that all of the infill houses in the various inner city neighbourhoods would be tendered in one package. ICR decided not to submit a bid as a tender for more than thirty units based on the lowest price was not in the company's best interest. First, in order to build that number of houses, ICR would need to significantly increase its staffing along with the necessary training and management supervision. It was also not compatible with ICR's commitment to ongoing year-round employment for its staff as an increase of this magnitude would probably be unsustainable. More importantly the tender for these houses in previous years had been awarded to a contractor at a very low price, significantly lower than the bids from all of the other contractors, including ICR. Prior to 2010, ICR was awarded a number of units in specific neighbourhoods at the price of the winning tender price that year; however, this practice was discontinued in 2010.

Commercial and Institutional Projects

ICR works not only on building new and renovating old houses and also takes on projects in the commercial and institutional sectors. Dilapidated and boarded-up houses affect available and suitable housing for people, while boarded-up commercial buildings are symptomatic of a deteriorating neighbourhood and affect the overall safety of the area. Commercial and institutional projects are important to ICR's social mandate, but they are also important to ICR as a business. Commercial projects provide more employment and training opportunities. The size of these projects often requires as many as ten or more workers over a long period of time. With the concentration of staff in one place it is easier to train people and supervise them. Large projects approaching a million dollars or more provide a steady cash flow and less need to continually source new work. They ease projections and worries about the future. Most importantly, however, the profit margins on commercial work are higher than projects related to social housing, with their very tight budgets.

Commercial and Institutional Projects on Selkirk Avenue

At ICR's start-up in 2002, Selkirk Avenue in the Winnipeg's North End was one long row of boarded-up commercial properties. As mentioned earlier, the block between Parr Street and Andrew Street had more than 70 percent of its buildings closed. Financial institutions, both banks and credit unions, had vacated the neighbourhood, and their properties were up for sale. Selkirk Avenue has a long and wonderful history. For many years it was the shopping destination for people from all parts of the city. Oretski department store, once the centre of this vibrant shopping street, was closed and crumbling from neglect. The Park Theatre, Clifford's clothing store, Woolworths department store and many more commercial properties were all shut down. Some of these properties served as warehouses and others were left to deteriorate. This block, once a hub of activity, felt like part of a ghost town. Due to the lack of people and boarded-up storefronts, the neighbourhood felt unsafe. Reports in the media about violent crime in the area did not help the situation. They encouraged people to stay away, especially at night after the few remaining commercial establishments closed up.

In 1999, Garry Loewen, the Manitoba staff organizer with the Mennonite Central Committee (MCC), mobilized community activists and local community organizations in an effort to try to collectively address these issues and turn the tide. The birth of the North End Community Renewal Corporation (NECRC) resulted from this effort. With the financial assistance of MCC, it purchased a building in the middle of the predominantly boarded-up block on Selkirk Avenue. By the time ICR commenced operations in 2002, NECRC had started to have an impact. The Oretski and Clifford properties had been demolished to make way for what has become the new extension campus for the University of Manitoba Faculty of Social Work. The boarded-up Woolworths store had been purchased by Urban Circle Training Centre Inc., a community-based not-for-profit organization providing pre-employment training and employment for Aboriginal women and men. They chose this new location to be part of the Selkirk Avenue renewal and to be in closer proximately to their student base.

In early 2003, ICR was hired as the major contractor on the Urban Circle Training Centre project. This was ICR's first attempt at commercial renovation, although it was perhaps premature for ICR to take on such a large and complicated project. In keeping with Aboriginal traditions and culture, the renovation included circular rooms, requiring multiple layers of thin drywall bent to the certain specifications. It also required large custom circular windows, an elevator, fireplace and a teepee structure in the middle of the building that rose from the basement through to the elevated roof. Completion of this highly visible project set the stage for ICR to become a major renovation contractor for commercial properties in the inner city.

Over the next few years, ICR was the contractor for many more projects on Selkirk Avenue. Projects included a major renovation to the Up Shoppe, a retail store that builds employment skills in local women, and the women's shelter accommodation units above the store, both sponsored by the North End Women's Centre. Another project was a renovation of what was originally part of the Indian Family Centre to create local community office space for the Winnipeg Regional Health Authority. It included a significant renovation project for NECRC, which had purchased the boarded-up retail space across the street from its own office. NECRC had acquired the property in part to contribute to the renewal and rejuvenation of Selkirk Avenue and in part as an investment strategy to lessen dependence on government grant funding. The provincial government entered into a long-term lease for this building with NECRC to set up the Murdo Scribe Centre, an Aboriginal training and employment centre. ICR was able to capitalize on its experience with the Urban Circle renovation as this project also included circular rooms.

ICR also renovated a closed up credit union building just west of Andrew Street, which had been purchased by the Elizabeth Fry Society as part of its expansion program. Unlike ICR's first commercial renovation experience with the Urban Circle project, it broke even or did better on these subsequent commercial projects.

By 2007, ICR had completed a dozen commercial projects on Selkirk Avenue and neighbouring streets including additional renovation projects for properties purchased by the North End Community Renewal Corporation, an overhaul to the Indian Family Centre, a significant repair to the building at the corner of Selkirk Avenue and McGregor Street owned by Oyata Tipi Cumini Yape, a not-for-profit that distributes used household goods and furniture to women and children trying to escape poverty and/or abusive situations. On Salter Avenue not far from Selkirk Avenue, ICR renovated the new home of Supporting Employment and Economic Development (SEED) Winnipeg, a not-for-profit agency that fights poverty and helps renew Winnipeg's inner city by assisting residents in starting up new businesses. These and other projects make ICR one of the major contributors to the area's renewal.

Commercial and Institutional Projects in Other Neighbourhoods

Armed with the learning and confidence gained from the early commercial renovations on Selkirk Avenue, ICR now takes on commercial projects around the city. These have been predominantly for not-for-profit organizations, many of which are in the Aboriginal community. Several major projects were completed for Southern Authority Child and Family Services, including Neechewan on Sherbrook Avenue, Ahsanook on Adele Avenue and its administrative offices on Portage Avenue. There were also projects for several daycares, including Eagle Wing Early Education Centre, Nigaanaki Daycare Centre and Little People's Place. In addition, there were renovation projects for senior residences and health centres. After completing a major renovation to the main administrative building for MacDonald Youth Services (MYS), ICR entered into a relationship with MYS to provide renovation upgrades on a number of its housing properties around the city.

ICR's renovation projects are not limited to not-for-profit organizations. In 2008, the architectural firm Bridgman Collaborative Architecture engaged ICR to both renovate and build a new addition onto the boarded-up Dominion Bank Building at Main Street and Higgins Avenue. The firm had recently purchased the heritage building for its own new offices on the main floor and rental space on the second floor. The addition included new entrance and staircase to access the second floor without having to go through the ground floor space. The project also included the installation of numerous large windows in what was previously a solid brick wall. This was not the first

Dominion Bank Building new home of Bridgman Collaborative Architecture

project where ICR took on new-build construction projects. A year earlier, ICR had been the framing contractor for a new Assiniboine Credit Union (ACU) branch on north Main Street. This was followed up with a second new branch for ACU on Pembina Highway in the south part of the city. The latter was a Leadership in Energy and Environmental Design (LEED) certified project. A year earlier, ICR had been the general contractor for another LEED certified project, renovating the third floor of the Mountain Equipment Co-op building on Portage Avenue. This floor provided office space for a number of Manitoba-based environmental organizations. In 2010, WinnipegRealtors decided to renovate its three-storey office building on Portage Avenue and chose ICR as its general contractor.

ICR's Role in Inner City Renewal

ICR's role in renewing Winnipeg's inner city infrastructure resulted in part from being at the right place at the right time. ICR started up and formed partnerships with local community organizations at a time when they be-ginning to take positive action to deal with community problems. Decaying buildings and boarded-up houses had to be addressed as an initial part of addressing the community problems of arson, crime, poverty, safety and proliferation of gangs.

ICR, with its employee base of local residents, is particularly well suited for this task. ICR's employees are familiar with and comfortable working in the community, their community. Since most employees do not own vehicles, it is easy for them to get to work by walking, bicycling or using public transportation, as they do not have long distances to travel. Those who do own vehicles often provide rides for their co-workers, and when necessary ICR's truck transports employees to jobsites that are not easily accessible. Working on local community projects creates an opportunity for friends, neighbours and relatives to witness the work by ICR employees. Employees take pride in their role in community rejuvenation and can be overheard saying things like "I worked on this project" and "I installed those windows." ICR employees are recognized as role models to others in the community, prompting many others to try to obtain employment at ICR.

There are other reasons why ICR is particularly suited to take on this task of inner city renewal. In discussions with private contractors, I learned that they were reluctant to participate in the community infrastructure renewal because of low profit margins, security of the construction sites and perceived fear for the personal safety of their employees. As long as there is plenty of work available on private commercial and residential renovation projects, associated with higher profit margins in other parts of the city, private sector construction companies are less interested in taking on projects in the inner city. The condition of most of the derelict houses prior to renovation also a concern as they were often dirty, stinky and full of remnants from tenants who in some cases had vacated years earlier. In combination, these factors have created an opportunity for ICR's active participation in the infrastructure renewal of Winnipeg's inner city, especially the North End.

Mountain Equipment Co-op Building in downtown Winnipeg

The foregoing also points out the main difference between private enterprise and a social enterprise. A social enterprise is motivated by and is pursuing its social mission while the private enterprise is pursuing profit. Both may be engaged in community renewal and rejuvenation but they are motivated in totally different ways. This is not to say that a social enterprise can be indifferent to financial sustainability; at the end of the day it needs to be profitable to be socially useful and responsible, but it cannot sacrifice its social mission and community involvement for profit.

Safety

The renewal of derelict properties in the inner city has a direct impact on safety in the community, as well as on the incidence of arson because the easy targets of boarded-up properties are removed. More importantly, however, residents have started to take pride in their community. As the property values begin to rise, homeowners make improvements to their homes. Open shops with storefront windows instead of plywood hoarding create a sense of safety as people become aware that they could be seen from these premises. New stores and institutional buildings also increase the number of pedestrians on commercial streets, creating both perceived and real safety.

Local Economy

As mentioned earlier, during its first eight years, ICR paid out more than $3 million in wages and benefits to its employees. As most of the employees live in the local community, a portion of their income is spend on local housing. With limited access to the outer reaches of the city, they purchase most of their life necessities such as food and clothing in the inner city. To the extent that there is any discretional income, most of that is also spent in the local community.

In addition to the wages and benefits to its employees during those years, ICR paid another $3 million to its subcontractors (electricians, plumbers, roofers, flooring and concrete specialists), the majority of which were small local businesses. Add to this the purchase of building materials (lumber, panel products, fasteners, siding, windows and doors, tiles, flooring, paint, etc.) for another $3 million, and you have most of ICR's revenue being spent in the local community. This approach and commitment to community economic development sets a social enterprise apart from a private enterprise, which pursues subcontractors and supplies from the lowest bidder or source. ICR supports McDiarmid Lumber, a building supply distributor headquartered in Winnipeg, and purchases its windows from a small local manufacturer adjacent to its own space on Dufferin Avenue. Flooring is bought from a couple of local independent businesses, one of which is only a few blocks away on Salter Street. It is this kind of spending that is so critical to community economic development. Many private and large contractors have employees who live outside the area, and they purchase supplies from major, often international, chains located on the city perimeter. These kind of hiring and purchasing practices result in "leakage" (as economists put it) of money from the local community.

Another way that ICR participates in and supports community economic development is as a member of the local social purchasing portal. The portal is an opportunity to foster local community economic development. Its members are committed to providing and purchasing goods and services among the portal's participants. A good example of this reciprocal relationship was ICR and Neechi Foods Co-op, a North End grocery store less than a kilometre away from ICR's offices. ICR purchases food and catering services for its meetings and celebrations from Neechi, and in return Neechi purchased renovation/repair services for its aging store on Dufferin Street from ICR.

ICR's longevity and success is a model for other social enterprises in the local community and elsewhere across Canada. Locally, BUILD (Building Urban Industries for Local Development) followed in ICR's footsteps as a social enterprise not-for-profit contractor and a training program for people who face barriers to employment. Over the years, ICR and BUILD have co-operated and supported each other, especially with staffing. During slow times at ICR, some staff worked on BUILD projects, and as BUILD's employees were trained and wanted to pursue a carpentry career they moved to ICR. Nationally, ICR and BUILD are both role models for social enterprise development in the construction industry. Community organizations in Brandon, Manitoba, and St John's, Newfoundland/Labrador, have set up social enterprises based on the BUILD model, while community organizations in Toronto and Calgary are pursuing social enterprises based on the ICR model.

ICR shares its experience with other organizations interested in starting social enterprises regardless of sector. Informally, ICR's business plan, newsletters, social return on investment (SROI) reports and other information are on its website. On a formal basis, as ICR's general manager, I participated as a member on the Urban Aboriginal Economic Development National Network research project, which emphasized the potential role for social enterprises in Aboriginal urban economic development. I was also invited to give presentations on social enterprise at numerous CED conferences, including the annual local CED Gathering in Winnipeg, and the national social enterprise conferences. As a founding member of the Social Enterprise Council of Canada, I participated in programs at international social enterprise forums in Edinburgh and San Francisco.

ICR's influence and role is not limited to social enterprises and the social economy. ICR is an active participant in a group of local socially conscious business owners that discusses, explores and shares management ideas on how to remain competitive and be successful in a changing environment. Al Dueck, President and CEO of Duxton Windows, was instrumental in providing leadership and coordination for this group of local community business leaders. The group included an architect, a business professor, a community organization executive director, a self-employed inventor, and a handful of small business owners and met on a monthly basis usually over breakfast a local hotel. The goal was to learn from each other's successes and challenges. This initiative was quite innovative as it brought together both social and private sector entrepreneurs as well as community activists to exchange experiences and ideas.

Real Community Development and Involvement

ICR is deeply involved in its community and in the development of its community. ICR consciously chose community building as part of its social mission. This includes a commitment to employing people who lived in Winnipeg's North End and to focusing its building and procurement in the inner city and taking part in North End organizations. This means that ICR participates in circulating money within the North End. This conscious and socially motivated strategy points out the difference between private enterprise and social enterprise participation in the community. Conventional capitalist private enterprise pursues profits, participating in community building when it coincides with its own best interest. One of the main economic problems with community economic development by outsiders is that they actually "leak" economic resources out of those communities. For private enterprise, community involvement is often part of a marketing tool and is incidental to their main mandate of maximizing shareholder profit.

Note

1.   Deane 2006.

Chapter 6

Impact on the Broader Community

In addition to participating in the infrastructure and social renewal in local inner city communities, ICR also participates in the broader community. ICR has had an impact on all three government levels — federal, provincial and municipal. In the public sector, ICR in effect delivers social services such as job training and community infrastructure improvement. On this social policy level, ICR illustrates that social enterprises can be an effective way of dealing with poverty and its consequences. ICR's positive effect extends to government finances. As a social enterprise ICR is cost effective in achieving community, provincial and national social goals; in fact, ICR actually provides a net financial benefit on the government investment in it. On the broadest social level, ICR is a model strategy to create a more just and equitable society. The notion that a more equal community affects everyone in the community, not just the disadvantaged, is worth restating while discussing the social policy impacts.

Government Social Economic Policy

ICR and other social enterprises have raised the profile of social enterprises in Canada but had little impact when it came to setting new federal social enterprise/social economy policy leading up to 2010. Unlike national governments in the United Kingdom, Italy and other European countries where governments developed specific legislation and policies to support and enhance the role of social enterprises in the economy, Canada is still in the exploration and research stage, starting to look at how government can provide assistance and encouragement.

In its February 2004 Speech from the Throne, the Government of Canada identified the "social economy" as a federal priority. Subsequently, in its budget for the year, it allocated $132 million for initiatives to support the social economy in terms of capacity building, financing and research. It also committed to improving the access of social enterprises to programs and services for small and medium sized enterprises. The capacity building and capital funds were disbursed in Quebec, but withdrawn for the rest of Canada by the new Conservative government of Stephen Harper.

In 2008, a few social economy activists, including myself, were invited to Ottawa to give a presentation to Human Resource Development Canada (HRDC) senior staff responsible for developing national social policies. The thirty or so staff in attendance seemed impressed with the potential related to social enterprises and asked numerous questions. They were aware that other countries had developed social and economic policies to support the creation and sustainability of social enterprises. The U.K., for instance, has a government department dedicated to the development of social enterprises, supports organizations set up to assist social enterprises and adopted community benefit clauses in the procurement of government goods and services. To date, however, the federal government in Canada has done little in the way of specific legislation and policy development.

Some provincial governments have developed and implemented programs supportive to social enterprises, and some have provided financial assistance to social enterprises. Both Manitoba and Nova Scotia have set up a tax credit programs to encourage investment in community enterprises, including social enterprises. The Community Enterprise Development Tax Credit Program in these two provinces offers individuals a 30 percent tax credit up for an annual investment of up to $30,000.

Job Creation

All levels of government are interested in the development of new small enterprises and the associated job creation. It is well known that small enterprises, those with five to a hundred employees, play a significant role in the Canadian economy. They account for 98 percent of all businesses, 48.3 percent of Canada's workforce and 42 percent of Canada's gross domestic product (GDP) in 2005.[1] Job creation stimulates the economy, increases tax revenues and decreases unemployment and social assistance expenditures. Governments, therefore, are willing to spend significantly on job creation. An HRDC study in 1986 evaluated multiple job creation programs. The Canadian Employment Strategy NTEP program was the highest cost, at $49,000 per job, and the Canadian Employment Strategy LEAP program was the least costly, at $4,200 per job created. Adjusting these figures to 2011 dollars, it costs government between $7,676 and $88,155 to create one job in Canada.[2] On a provincial level, the Ontario government in 2010 entered into a commitment with Samsung to pay $437 million to the company to create 16,000 factory jobs over a twenty-five year period. This works out to $27,312 per job.[3]

The cost of job creation at ICR falls easily within this range of job creation costs. Assuming that the total amount of government funding excluding job-training funding went towards job creation, it works out that the cost of creating one job at ICR was just under $17,000. This is based on creating thirty full-time permanent jobs at ICR with $500,000 funding from government. In fact, not all of the government funding was related to job creation as a significant portion was intended to provide social supports to ICR's employees. Therefore the cost of creating one job at ICR was actually significantly less than $17,000.

Social Service Delivery

Social enterprises have taken on, or fallen into, a role in the delivery of social services and programs. This role is manifested in two ways. One is "internal," to the enterprise and is related to social services such as job training and health benefits provided to its employees. The other is "external," where social enterprises provide a social service in the community that is usually provided by government, such as home care, care of the aged, child welfare, foreign aid and so on. A good example of external social service delivery is youth services delivered by RAY (Resource Assistance for Youth) in Winnipeg. This external provision of social services has increased with recent economic hard times as governments cut back social services as way to deal with large deficits caused by other circumstances.

It is very tempting for governments, which are trying to balance their budgets, to encourage social enterprises to provide both internal and external social service delivery. Although social enterprises which provide internal social supports can absorb some of the related costs, they cannot sustain all of the costs. They require some incentives from government either in the form of tax breaks or grants to offset the additional costs related to providing these social services. There is some speculation that social enterprises can provide certain social programs and supports, both internal and external, more effectively than government.

ICR is an internal social service delivery social enterprise. Moreover, the internal supports provided by ICR are holistic, combining job training, health benefits and social support, and are not focused on a single issue like many government social programs. Some critics might claim that ICR is really just delivering a job-readiness program for government. I disagree with that characterization, in large part because ICR did not actually cost the government anything.

A number of social enterprises, including ICR, provide training as part of their social mission. At any one time, approximately 75 percent of ICR's employees are engaged in on-the-job training, albeit at different levels. Training costs are calculated annually by assigning portions of supervisors'/trainers' wages and assigning productivity ratios to different levels of trainees. The informal annual training costs for ICR are estimated to be $100,000 to $120,000 (approximately $5,000 per trainee). Much of these training costs were absorbed internally by ICR.

By 2005, the Manitoba provincial government recognized ICR's role in skill training and started to provide an annual $50,000 training grant, representing approximately 50 percent of ICR's annual training costs. It is important to note that this training grant is available to any enterprise in the private sector, but it had previously not been accessed by a social enterprise. On-the-job training is a cost-effective training method as it leverages other internal ICR resources, such as management and administrative costs. In addition to the informal training expenses, ICR paid for registration and books for employees entering into the formal provincial apprenticeship training programs at Red River College. Based on an annual enrolment of three to four employees, the related cost for the formal training is approximately $1,500 per year.

Over the years, ICR has had a significant impact on skill training. All eligible ICR employees are encouraged to pursue official apprenticeship training, with the company picking up the associated costs. Many employers in the construction trades are reluctant to support apprenticeship training for their employees as they not only lose the employees for ten weeks each year, but upon completion of each level the apprentice has to be paid at the official rate for the level achieved. This rate is usually higher than the rate for employees with the same skill set who are not registered in the formal apprenticeship program. As reported earlier in this book, in 2008, the Apprenticeship Board named ICR as "Employer of the Year" for its role and commitment to apprenticeship training.

Benefits accruing to government are not limited to training. Health and housing related assistance provided by ICR also have positive impacts on the provincial government. The ICR employee health benefit plan, along with better nutrition from having sufficient income, must have a positive effect on employees' general health, thus potentially reducing health related expenses for government. Similarly, ICR's support for access to better, affordable housing has the potential to reduce health related expenses as living conditions improve.

The role of social enterprises in the local economy has not had much attention from municipal governments, including the City of Winnipeg, even though ICR's role in social housing, employment creation and training benefitted the local community and municipal government. As documented earlier, ICR was also instrumental in renovating boarded-up houses, rejuvenating commercial areas, reducing arson and creating a safer, more livable community. Perhaps more importantly from the city's perspective, the overall contributions by ICR enhanced the quality of life in the city, especially in the inner city.

Government Funding

There has been some controversy related to government funding support to social enterprises like ICR. For example, some critics claim that social enterprises are really nothing more than disguised government programs and as such do not "pay" for themselves. During its first eight years, ICR, via COS, received funding support from both the provincial and federal governments. In 2002, the Manitoba government provided COS with $250,000 spread over four years (2002–05), as part of the Neighbourhood Alive initiative to assist

COS with its poverty alleviation strategy. Then in 2006, it received $250,000 spread over four years (2006–09) from the Winnipeg Partnership Agreement. The agreement was signed in May 2004 and represented a five-year, $75 million commitment by the governments of Canada, Manitoba and Winnipeg to strengthen neighbourhoods, promote economic development and enable Aboriginal citizens to fully participate in Winnipeg's economic and social opportunities. At the municipal level, Winnipeg assisted ICR with its role in the Affordable Housing and Homelessness Initiative, which funded the inner city social housing agencies important to ICR's early years. Although ICR received government funding particularly in its early years, ICR has gradually and consistently increased its earned revenue ratio (revenue from operations as a percentage of total revenue including grants) throughout the 2002–10 period. By 2010 its earned revenue ratio was more than 95 percent. This compares very favourably with the average earned revenue ratio among social enterprises in Canada.

Impact on Government Finances

ICR has had a positive financial impact on all three levels of government. In renovating dilapidated properties in the city core, ICR plays a role in increasing municipal property tax revenues. This increase is not limited to previously boarded-up residential and commercial properties but comes also from increased property values of existing houses and businesses resulting from the general improvement in the surrounding community. In a span of eight years, from 2002 to 2010, residential property values more than doubled in the city core.[4] Some of this increase is attributable to ICR and other community organizations involved in community infrastructure renewal.

In addition, as pointed out earlier, ICR has had a positive effect on safety in the inner city, thereby reducing pressures on policing and fire fighting resources. Although it is difficult to come up with hard numbers for some of these impacts, I estimate that over the eight-year span, ICR along with other social enterprises were responsible for a small positive impact on the city's finances. ICR's role and its modest impact has gone mostly unnoticed by city officials.

ICR is also responsible for net positive financial impacts at the provincial and federal government levels. ICR's job creation has a combined impact of increasing government revenue while decreasing government expenditures (this is discussed in more detail below in Social Return on Investment). As a company, ICR makes employer contributions to the Canadian Pension Plan (CPP) and paid Goods and Services Tax (GST) on goods and services purchased as part of doing business.

In addition, individual ICR employees pay personal income tax to both levels of government on their total earnings, which over an eight-year period totaled in excess of $3 million. They also make employee contributions to Canada Pension Plan and to Employment Insurance. I also expect that a considerable amount of ICR employees' earned income is spent on purchases with the associated PST, GST and other taxes. This is new revenue generation for the government, considering that many of ICR's employees were previously unemployed, drawing funds from the federal employment insurance program or drawing funds from the provincial social assistance program. ICR's employees with a criminal record are far less likely to re-offend, thereby making a positive impact on policing, justice system and penal system costs.

The financial impact on government revenues and expenditures related to providing gainful employment varies with the background and history of the individual. In the worst-case scenario, related to an offender, the annual cost of keeping a person incarcerated in a federal prison was $87,665 in 2005.[5] Add to this the cost related to the policing and court cases during the arrest and prosecution, and the total cost is considerably higher. This same person employed and making ICR's average wage of $15 per hour generates an annual income of $31,200, on which the person pays personal income tax.

No matter how one calculates the financial impacts of ICR on government, it is always positive as people move from being a drain on the public purse to making a contribution. A few scenarios illustrate this point. The scenario analysis is based on 2010 actual figures and conservative assumptions. All of the scenarios are based on ICR average annual gross earnings of $31,200 ($15 average hourly rate for non journeyperson crew members).

Scenario 1: Financial impact on government based on a single person who is employed by ICR but previously incarcerated in a federal prison for the entire year.

Tax revenue generated for provincial and federal governments	
Federal Income Tax on taxable earnings of $22,000 @ marginal TR 15%	$3,300
Prov. Income Tax on taxable earnings of $22,000 @ marginal TR 10.8%	$2,376
GST paid on $10,000 expenditures @5%	$500
PST paid on $10,000 expenditures @ 7%	$700
Total tax revenue generated to both levels of government	$6,876
Less provincial training grant $50,000 for all employee training	$5,000
Expenses saved by provincial and federal governments:	
One year Incarceration	$95,730
Net gain for government	$97,606

Scenario 2: Financial impact on government based a person with three dependents (spouse and two children). Person employed by ICR was previously unemployed and collected EI for part of the year and social assistance for the remainder of the year.

Tax revenue generated for government	
Federal Income Tax on taxable earnings of $10,000 @ marginal TR 15%	$1,500
Prov. Income Tax on taxable earnings of $10,000 @ marginal TR 10.8%	$1,080
GST paid on $10,000 expenditures @5%	$500
PST paid on $10,000 expenditures @ 7%	$700
Total tax revenue generated to both levels of government	$3,780
Less provincial training grant $50,000 for all employee training	$5,000
Expenses saved by provincial and federal governments	
Maximum EI payout (26 weeks @ $275)	$7,150
Social assistance for the balance of the year (26 weeks @ $413)	$10,738
Skill Training related costs	$5,000
Total expenses saved by government	$22,888
Net gain for government	$21,668

Scenario 3: Financial impact on government based on person with multiple dependents employed by ICR who was previously on multi-year (generational) social assistance.

Revenue generated for provincial and federal governments	
Federal Income Tax on taxable earnings of $5,000 @ marginal TR 15%	$750
Prov. Income Tax on taxable earnings of $ 5,000 @ marginal TR 10.8%	$540
GST paid on $10,000 expenditures @5%	$500
PST paid on $10,000 expenditures @ 7%	$700
Total tax revenue generated to both levels of government	$2,490
Less provincial training grant $50,000 for all employee training	$5,000
Expenses saved by government	
Social assistance for (52 weeks @ $500)	$26,000
Total expenses saved by government	$26,000
Net gain for government	$23,490

In all three of the above scenarios reflecting circumstances related to ICR employees in 2010, there was a net savings to government for any given employee ranging from $21,688 to $97,606. Some of the ICR employees had been on social assistance for generations while others were unemployed and collecting EI the year before joining ICR. Assuming that in 2010, ten out of the thirty ICR employees fell into the employee target group described in the three scenarios, the net savings to government for that one year would range from $216,680 to $976,060, depending on the ratio of employees in each category. These savings do not reflect intangible or hard-to-estimate impacts related to policing and the criminal justice system, social housing, food banks and the like.

Social Return on Investment

As a social enterprise with two bottom lines, financial and social, ICR needs to evaluate its performance related to these two goals on an annual basis. The financial performance measurement is similar to that of any private sector capitalist enterprise. An independent auditor reviews and analyzes the financial performance and prepares audited financial statements that are submitted to Revenue Canada and circulated to board members, financial institutions and funders. Socially minded investors like SCP, concerned with social impacts, are also interested in measuring and evaluating the social bottom line. SCP needed a performance measurement tool so that as investors they could understand the social enterprise business model, the challenges and trade offs. It would also provide a great platform to engage with COS and the ICR management team on performance management and strategic planning.

An evaluation of ICR's performance on its social objectives was difficult as there were no readily available templates for evaluating social performance. As ICR was starting out, SCP was developing the Social Return on Investment (SROI) model to evaluate performance related to social objectives. Joanne Norris, a staff person with SCP who was responsible for developing the model, used ICR as a test case. She drafted a questionnaire that was used with all staff in the first year of the enterprise to establish a base line for social indicators, including employee's health, housing situation and number of dependents. The interviews conducted by Joanne with the assistance of Larry Morrissette, ICR's social worker, were done in private and were confidential.

The first SROI report documented an overview of ICR's employees. It revealed that 79 percent were unemployed and 6 percent were receiving social assistance prior to starting work with ICR and only 37 percent had ever held a job for more than two years. It also revealed that only 11 percent had graduated from high school, 63 percent had dependent children, 58 percent had a criminal record and 47 percent used food bank services in the year prior to ICR employment.

In that first year, ending in July 31, 2003, a total investment of $368,000 in form of grants and subsidies had been raised to cover start-up costs, the operating loss and the costs associated with providing social supports. At the same time, the average change in societal contribution calculated by taking the annual social assistance of an individual before hire and subtracting annual income tax paid before hire and then adding the annual income tax paid after hire was $8,080. Based on average number of target employees of 18.5, the total change in the societal contribution was $149,500. Therefore the SROI for year one, calculated by taking the total change in societal contribution ($149,500) and dividing it by the total required investment ($368,000) was 41 percent.

The ongoing portion of societal contribution calculated by subtracting annual income tax paid before hire from annual income tax paid after hire was $74,000. The projected long term SROI, calculated by multiplying the ongoing portion of societal contribution ($74,000) by the annuity multiplier (assumed to be twelve years) divided by the total investment required ($368,000) was 241 percent. Copies of the complete SROI reports for the years ending July 31, 2003, and July 31, 2009, are in Appendix 4.

Over the next four years, Joanne Norris personally interviewed every ICR target employee. The evaluation documented individual employee progress related to housing, health, nutrition, training, domestic issues and a host of other parameters. This data was collated and reported on an integrated basis in an annual SROI report. The report also reviewed and documented financial investment along with the SROI mathematical calculation. Starting in year five, the task of interviewing, collecting and analyzing the SROI data was passed on to Reconnaissance Management Consulting Group Inc, which continued the exercise using the same format developed by SCP.

At the end of year seven, the total investment to date was $1,339,135 and the cumulative SROI was 55 percent. The cumulative cost savings to date had grown to $741,136. Approximately 33 percent of the original target employee base (low-income inner city residents) recruited in year one was still employed by ICR at the end of year seven. The SROI report was circulated along with the audited financial statements on an annual basis. The SROI reports are available on the company website.

The SROI report figures are not to be confused with the estimated financial returns to governments calculated earlier on in this chapter. The SROI calculations are based on all investment capital regardless of its source. It includes grants from foundations, corporations, community organizations like the United Way and individuals as well as government. The portion from government grants represents a fraction of the total capital investment.

The Private Sector

How does ICR or any social enterprise for that matter relate to the private sector? Most social enterprises provide real goods and services and compete with private sector enterprises in the main economy. However since most social enterprises are incorporated as not-for-profit organizations, they are not considered part of the private sector. In addition they are often marginalized due to their relatively small size. ICR however was incorporated as a for-profit enterprise, delivers a needed service, maintains a significant workforce and competes in the private sector. ICR illustrates that a social enterprise can find a balance and successfully deliver on both financial and social goals.

ICR is a good example of integrating social objectives into the everyday aspects of doing business. ICR illustrates that an enterprise, any enterprise including those in the private sector, can incorporate social objectives and be socially responsible and still make a profit. A number of entrepreneurs and managers in the private sector came to realize the potential impact of social enterprises. Bill Young, President and CEO of Social Capital Partners (SCP), championed the role of social enterprises in the private sector. In 2002, he set up an investment organization to support enterprises that create employment opportunities for people in challenging inner city communities. Since those early days, SCP has emerged as a significant organization in social investment and in the development of enterprises in the private sector that incorporate social objectives.

During the past few years, it has been recognized that incorporating social objectives into the traditional private sector businesses provides benefits to the enterprise, its employees and the entire community. This realization has not been lost on business schools, including those at the University of Winnipeg, York University and Acadia University in Canada as well as Harvard University in the United States, which now offer courses in social entrepreneurship and social enterprise. This is mainly due to the growing awareness about and interest in social issues among young business students and their desire to find a balance between financial and social goals as well as meaning and happiness in their lives.

There seems to be a realization that enterprises in the private sector as well as those in the social economy sector can play a significant role in dealing with social issues. In recent years, SCP has been committed to changing the hiring practices in private sector enterprises to provide access to people previously shut out. Entrepreneurs and business leaders have the added satisfaction that they are making a contribution to the social fabric of their community and not just to their shareholders, who are mainly interested in financial returns. I get the sense that for a growing segment of the business community, particularly young people, the amount of income that a person earns and the amount of wealth a person accumulates are no longer the only yardsticks for success in business and life. This may be indicated by the popularity of psychology professor Tal Ben-Shahar, at Harvard, who makes the argument that true happiness is found in life meaning. Approximately 20 percent of all recent graduates from Harvard have attended his course on positive psychology.[6]

The private sector media has also picked up on the role of and impacts of social enterprises and social entrepreneurs on the economy. ICR has been featured in local and national newspapers, television news programs and documentaries and magazines and journals. In 2009, the CBC featured ICR in the "Canadians Making a Difference" documentary series, broadcast on its news program *The National*. The program documented the impact of a social enterprise on a stressed community.

Also in 2009, Ernst and Young, a world leading management consulting firm, added social entrepreneur to the categories for the Entrepreneur of the Year award program. In 2010, in my capacity as ICR's general manager, I was a finalist for the Prairie region in the Canadian Entrepreneur of the Year competition and received a special recognition award at the national award dinner in Calgary.

As an active participant in the Winnipeg construction sector, ICR forms partnerships and business relationships with numerous private sector companies in the construction sector, sometimes in a sub contractor role but more often in the general contractor role, hiring private companies as subcontractors. ICR is a member and an active participant in various private sector construction related associations. On several occasions it entered its renovation projects in the annual Winnipeg Homebuilders Association renovation award competitions.

A Truly Public-Private Partnership

Both government and the private sector are positively affected by the emerging role of social enterprises in Canada, as shown by the experience of ICR. For government, ICR has a net positive financial impact — the investment made through grants and subsidies has been repaid many times over by reducing government expenses for the people who otherwise would not have good jobs and at the same time increasing net tax revenue. The community, particularly Winnipeg's North End, benefits from provision of economic and social services provided by ICR, such as adequate, affordable housing, but also from the spin-off effects of neighbourhood improvement. Individual entrepreneurs and corporate managers benefit as the pursuit of social objectives adds meaning to their lives. It is probably a widespread and well-accepted truism that lasting happiness requires a sense of meaning in one's life. There is also a benefit to society by creating a more equal society, to the extent that social justice objectives are included in all enterprises both in the social and private sectors. With all these benefits and potential benefits, the public investment in what are private, but social, enterprises can be a real partnership in pursuing the social good.

Notes

1. <http://www.cbc.ca/news/business/smallbusiness/story/2011/10/04/f-smallbiz-by-the-numbers.html>.
2. Roy and Wong 1990.
3. The Ontario provincial government entered into a multi-year agreement with Samsung providing grant funding related to jobs created in the province.
4. Average values increased from $40,000 more than $80,000. This is based on personal experience purchasing and selling properties in the North End.
5, Juristat, Statistics Canada at <http://www.vcn.bc.ca/august10/politics/facts_stats.html>.
6. Ben-Shahar 2007.

Part 4

CONTEXT AND ROLE

Chapter 7

The Social Economy

The "social economy" is that part of the economy which is not in either the public or private (for profit) sectors. It is also sometimes referred to as the "non-profit sector" or the "third sector." This sector consists of enterprises and organizations that are not in the public sector and whose primary goal is not to seek profit. Social enterprises, however, must be "profitable" to survive and remain competitive in a market-driven economy. Although the social economy sector has a long history, it really started to emerge in the mid 1970s as a worldwide economic crisis deepened and awareness developed about the limitations of the traditional public and private sectors.

The traditional social economy sector encompasses cooperatives, mutual societies and other associations. As social enterprises developed, they too became part of the social economy. Cooperatives can be either for-profit or not-for-profit organizations. A co-op is classified as producer, consumer, housing or worker depending on the constituency of its membership. Credit unions and caisse populaires are examples of financial co-ops. The worker co-op model is based on the workers as members and the enterprise operates for their benefit. Worker cooperatives in Winnipeg include Neechi Foods Co-op, Mondragon Café and Bookstore, and Organic Planet Foods. Mutual societies, sometimes referred to as "benevolent societies" or "fraternal organizations," are associations for the purposes of insurance, pensions or savings. A local example in Winnipeg's inner city is the Ukrainian Mutual Benefit Association. Associations include non-profit groups, voluntary organizations, non-governmental organizations, foundations and various types of charities. The Winnipeg Foundation, a local charity in Winnipeg, supports the needs of the community. Legal forms of incorporation and related tax laws for organizations in the social economy vary depending on jurisdiction.

A widely accepted international definition of the social economy developed by Defourny and others[1] states that the social economy includes economic activities carried out by cooperatives and related enterprises, mutual societies and associations whose ethical stance is represented by the following principles:

- a primary aim of serving members or the community, rather than generating profit;
- an independent management;
- a democratic decision-making process; and

- the primacy of people and labour over capital in the distribution of income.

In Canada, the social economy has developed mainly in Quebec, where it has a long history. The Chantier de l'économie sociale is an innovation bringing together many sectors and citizens groups in Quebec committed to building a social economy.[2] This organization accepted the definition by Defourny and added a fifth principle: that of participation, empowerment and responsibility, both individual and collective.

In the Canadian context, Quarter, Mook and Armstrong define the social economy as a bridging concept for organizations that have social objectives central to their mission and their practice, and either have explicit economic objectives or generate some economic value through the services they provide and purchases that they undertake.[3]

Non-profit organizations, mutual societies and cooperatives have increased their presence across the country, with the possible exception of Alberta. Worker cooperatives in particular have multiplied across the country with the benefit of the advocacy work by the Canadian Worker Co-op Federation. Social enterprises have started to develop across Canada with support from the Enterprising Non-Profits Program and advocacy work by the Social Enterprise Council of Canada.

Social Enterprises

Social enterprises, also sometimes referred to as social business enterprises, social firms, non-profit enterprises, social purpose businesses, social ventures, special purpose businesses and community businesses, are the latest development in the social economy sector. With their commitment to financial sustainability, pursuit of social goals and dedication to innovation, social enterprises encompass a new social and entrepreneurial spirit. Social enterprises are a contrast to private sector enterprises, which are committed mainly to maximizing profits for its shareholders or private owners. Social enterprises must be financially sound in order to be sustainable and continue to fulfill their social mandate. Financial surpluses/profits are reinvested in the community rather than distributed to a private owner or distant shareholder.[4]

There are different types of social enterprises, and definitions of social enterprise vary. Jacques Defourny, professor of economics at the University of Liege and director of the Centre for Social Economy in Belgium, identifies six types of social enterprises: those that integrate disabled people, those that integrate excluded people, those that are based on fair trade, those that address poverty alleviation, those that provide a service to the community and those that strengthen the social fabric. In general, social enterprises are designed to assist groups on the margins of society and to fight against social exclusion.[5]

Social enterprise definitions vary by region and organization.

> Social enterprises are businesses owned by nonprofit organizations, that are directly involved in the production and/or selling of goods and services for the blended purpose of generating income and achieving social, cultural, and/or environmental aims. Social enterprises are one more tool for non-profits to use to meet their mission to contribute to healthy communities. —Social Enterprise Council of Canada[6]

> Social enterprises are businesses whose primary purpose is the common good. They use the methods and disciplines of business and the power of the marketplace to advance their social, environmental and human justice agendas. — Social Enterprise Alliance, U.S.A.[7]

> A social enterprise is a business that trades for a social and/or environmental purpose. It will have a clear sense of its "social mission": which means it will know what difference it is trying to make, who it aims to help, and how it plans to do it. It will bring in most or all of its income through selling goods or services. And it will also have clear rules about what it does with its profits, reinvesting these to further the "social mission." — Social Enterprise, U.K. [8]

The European Research Network (EMES) includes the following parameters in its definition: A continuous activity producing goods and or selling services; a high degree of autonomy; a significant level of economic risk; a minimum amount of paid work; an explicit aim to benefit the community; an initiative launched by a group of citizens; a decision-making power not based on capital ownership; a participatory nature involving the persons affected by the activity; and limited profit distribution.[9]

Social enterprises may define themselves using their own terms, yet all will talk about the main elements that characterize a social enterprise:

- a continuous activity producing goods and or selling services. There has to be an economic activity with monetary exchanges;
- social objectives as the main reason for the business;
- profits/surpluses are for the benefit of the enterprise or its sponsoring non-profit organization, not for individuals or private shareholders;
- upon dissolution, assets are distributed to the community rather than to private shareholders; and
- pursuit of blended returns on investment between financial and social, not just financial.

The above elements make no reference to legal status or whether the social enterprise is a for-profit or not-for-profit enterprise. These elements can apply to both types of enterprise and can be incorporated into shareholder agreements of for-profit social enterprises.

Incorporation, Legal and Tax Issues

In Canada, social enterprises can be incorporated as non-share capital corporations (not-for-profit), share capital corporations (for-profit) or cooperatives under the *Cooperatives Act* (either for-profit or not-for-profit).

Some organizations, like Enterprising Non Profits (ENP), define social enterprises in part based on their incorporation status, for example, non-share capital corporations (these are corporations without ownership shares and are by definition not-for-profit organizations) while other organizations, like Social Enterprise in the United Kingdom and organizations in most of the other European Union countries, make no reference to legal status or profit motive. The fact that there is no specific legal entity for social enterprise is not a deterrent to the establishment of social enterprises; in fact it could be a blessing as organizations may choose their preferred incorporation model and profit related status. If employee ownership is part of the social mission, then the share capital corporation (corporation with ownership shares and for-profit motive) or worker cooperative are the only two incorporation options. Those that pursue social enterprises in the context of the non-share capital (not-for-profit) incorporation status, either within an existing or new not-for- profit organization, can do so as long as the enterprise is related to the mission of the not-for-profit organization. This option also applies to not-for-profits with charitable status. In the Canadian legal context, mission "related" businesses are allowed for non-profits and charities.

In Canada, the surplus or profit generated by a social enterprise is taxed differently depending on whether it is incorporated as a for-profit or not-for-profit corporation or cooperative. For-profit corporations have to pay corporate income tax on their profits while not-for-profit corporations are not taxed on any surplus. Surplus in not-for-profit organizations must be retained in the corporation for future use to achieve its mission. For-profit enterprises, however, can transfer up to 75 percent of their profit to a not-for-profit charitable corporation without a tax liability.[10]

Governance and Leadership

All corporations — share capital (for-profit), non-share capital (not-for-profit), cooperatives — are required by corporate law to have a board of directors. The board is a collective body that governs and provides strategic leadership for the organization. Boards of directors, including those for social enterprises, have three types of responsibilities: fiduciary, strategic and generative.

Fiduciary duties deal with compliance requirements, such as preventing misuse of resources and ensuring that board members act in the best interest of the enterprise; strategic responsibilities are related to discovering and setting strategic direction; and generative duties are related to reflection on leadership practice, to discover issues and make sense of them.

Typically, the duties of boards of directors include the following:

- governing the organization by establishing broad policies and objectives;
- selecting, appointing, supporting and reviewing the performance of the chief executive officer;
- ensuring the availability of adequate financial resources;
- approving annual budgets;
- accounting to the stakeholders for the organization's performance; and
- setting the salaries and compensation of company management.

In most Canadian jurisdictions individual board members are liable for the organization's unpaid wages and benefits as well as any outstanding amounts owing to Revenue Canada for source deductions. In addition to financial liability, board members can also be liable for not fulfilling their fiduciary responsibilities.

Effective leadership in a social enterprise is critical to its sustainability. Leadership is divided between the board of directors and the CEO or executive director. This shared responsibility can create tensions when the board and the CEO or executive director do not share the same values or vision for the direction of the enterprise. In situations where the CEO was also a founder of the social enterprise, the board may give the CEO too much liberty and provide inadequate scrutiny. Strong entrepreneurial leaders, like leaders in other areas, often possess charisma and passion. They tend to lead by example, take limited risks, overcome obstacles and hire the right people. They also invest in their own development and balance making money with the social mission.

Funding and Finance

Although the funding requirements for social enterprises are not that dissimilar to funding requirements in the private sector, the sources of funds are different. Private sector enterprises primarily rely on personal funds, family and angel investors for equity, especially in the start-up phase. For credit they rely on loans from traditional lenders. Once established, they rely on equity investment from venture capital funds and, for some, once established and successful, equity investment from a public offering on the stock exchange.

None of these sources are available to social enterprises. They are mainly dependent on grants from foundations and community organizations like the United Way. They also solicit donations from supportive people in the community. Some equity investment maybe accessed from social venture capital funds or from private investors purchasing non-voting preferred shares. Loans are by and large mainly available from community loan funds that offer "patient capital." Characteristics of patient capital in reference to the social enterprise sector include a willingness to forego maximum financial returns for social impact, greater tolerance for risk, longer time horizons for return of the capital and intensive support of management as they grow their enterprise. Once the enterprise has established some equity, it may be eligible for secured loans from a traditional financial institution. Both private and social enterprises require access to working capital. Lines of credit extended by financial institutions are usually based on the outstanding receivables of the enterprise.

Social enterprises may also receive some public funding to support initiatives related to job creation, training and employee assistance. However, the financial assistance by governments provided to social enterprises is just a small fraction of the government grants and loan guarantees to enterprises in the private corporate sector. Corporate capitalist and small capitalist enterprises rely heavily on public funding — from the hidden subsidies of such things as roads, public health and government-funded research to direct subsidies and grants.

In a couple of Canadian provinces, governments have set up tax credits for investment in community enterprises. In Manitoba, it is called the Community Enterprise Tax Credit and it allows individuals to claim a 30 percent tax credit for investments of up to $30,000 per year. Again this community enterprise (social enterprise) tax credit is tiny compared to the various tax credits supporting investment in the private sector.

Marketing

Marketing is a step in the process of getting an enterprise's product or service to the customer. It is just as important for social enterprises as it is for private sector enterprises as both are competing for sales in the marketplace. The four fundamentals which form the foundation of a marketing plan are product, place, price and promotion. The quality of the product, the dependability of the service, the distribution channel, competitive price and a sound promotion strategy are all key factors of a successful marketing strategy. Social enterprises are often tempted to lead with a promotion strategy focused on its social mission. It tries to attract potential customers by appealing to their sense of community and justice for the disadvantaged. This may work well in some sectors, for instance, manufacturing, where there is little or no contact between the buyer and the employees of the social enterprise. ImagineAbility Incorporated, a Winnipeg-based social enterprise with up to 400 employees, most of whom have an intellectual disability, takes full advantage of its social mission in its marketing. It is communicated to the institutional buyers and retail distributors as well as proudly displayed on the product packaging. Private sector enterprises often try to use their community involvement in their promotion strategies for the same reason.

Although this marketing approach seems to be effective for social enterprises in the manufacturing sector, it may be a liability in other sectors. The experience of two successful social enterprises operating in the service industry, Potluck Catering in Vancouver's Downtown East Side and Inner City Renovation in Winnipeg's North End, indicates that customers are more concerned about quality, service and price than they are about the enterprise's social mission.[11] This is counterintuitive to most people involved in marketing social enterprise products or services. However, experience shows that employing people with challenging backgrounds conjures up a negative impression among potential customers of services. Consequently, these social enterprises in the service sector must develop a marketing strategy that emphasizes quality, dependability and competitive pricing and only focus on its social mission with selected customers. Testimonials and word-of-mouth promotion tend to be effective marketing tools for social enterprises, especially those in the service sector. A social enterprise has the choice to prominently display and lead with the social mission, make reference to it along with other attributes or ignore it and concentrate on the basics in the marketing strategy. Ignoring the social mission may be a better choice for a social enterprise in the service sector with target employees that have a history with addictions, criminal activity and/or incarceration.

Social Enterprise Development in Canada

There is a long history of social enterprises in Canada, although the early forms were not recognized by that name. Some co-ops, like The People's Co-op in Winnipeg, founded in the 1928, were in fact social enterprises.[12] Some of the community non-profit organizations engaged in the delivery of social services for a fee were early pioneers of social enterprises.

Situated in Winnipeg, Versatech Industries Inc. (now ImagineAbility Inc.), which employs people with intellectual disabilities, started up in 1962. This social enterprise manufactures parts for customers that include Boeing and packages products for Coghlan's Ltd., a world leader in outdoor camping accessories. The Saskatchewan Association of Rehabilitation Centres (SARC), which provides recycling services across Saskatchewan, was established in 1968 and currently has more than 2000 employees. The Big Carrot Co-op, a retail health food store located in Toronto, started up as a worker cooperative with nine founding members in 1983. In 2012, nearly thirty years later, it has more than seventy worker owners and a total staff of well over a hundred people. Not all employees are members as there is a probationary period for new members. Engaged in the retail trade, The Big Carrot also has some part-time staff that may not meet the minimum weekly or annual time requirements to qualify for membership.

Social enterprises participate in various sectors of the economy, including fair trade products, recycling, restaurants and catering, retail sales, couriering, property management and construction. Many of the social enterprises across Canada tend to be relatively small, with fewer than twenty employees. Most social enterprises have been quite innovative in the development of their products and in the delivery of their services. A-Way Express in Toronto developed a courier delivery service based solely on using public transportation. The social enterprise kidsLINK, based in St. Agatha, Ontario, which provides services for kids and youth, has developed innovative entrepreneurial programs. ICR's approach to partnering with community housing organizations is an example of innovation in the delivery of a service. Finding a market niche and a competitive advantage is critical to success of a social enterprise.

Social Enterprise Networks

In 1997, an organization called Enterprising Non Profits (ENP), started up in British Columbia to support the development of social enterprises in that province. Over the past fifteen years, this organization has assisted hundreds of social enterprises with both financial and technical supports. In recent years ENP has expanded into Nova Scotia, Ontario, Alberta and Manitoba.

Another organization supporting the development of social enterprises in Canada is the Canadian CED Network (CEDNET). Originally concentrating on community economic development issues and organizations, by 2000, it started to take an active interest social enterprises and their development, and in the summer of 2011, CEDNET commissioned a social enterprise survey.[13] A total of 118 social enterprises across Manitoba were surveyed in an effort to develop clear indicators of the sector's size, market activities and socio-economic impacts. In 2010, these 118 social enterprises generated $55.4 million in revenue, including at least $41.5 million in sales. They paid about $25.3 million in wages and salaries to 3,750 people, 3,450 of whom were employed as part of the mission of the enterprise. This report builds a strong case for all stakeholders to value the distinct contributions of social enterprises and to work together in creating a supportive environment in which the sector can grow. This report builds on similar research conducted on the social enterprise sectors in British Columbia and Alberta. Research projects are also underway in Ontario and Eastern Canada in an effort to measure and quantify the impacts of social enterprises across Canada. CEDNET continues to support social enterprise development with policy papers, workshops and technical assistance.

In 2008, a group of social enterprise entrepreneurs and social activists founded the Social Enterprise Council of Canada (SECC). The council is an alliance of social enterprise leaders who leverage their networks, knowledge and experience in order to build a strong and enabling environment for social enterprises in Canada. The council has organized national social enterprise forums attracting a large number of people around the country. It has also been involved in the planning and delivery of annual world social enterprise forums. The first one, in 2008, was held in Edinburgh. Subsequent world forums took place in Melbourne, San Francisco, Johannesburg, Rio de Janeiro, and, in 2013, Calgary. These forums attract large numbers of participants, upwards of 1000 people attend.

Community loan funds are another network supportive to the development of social enterprise across Canada. These loan funds have sprung up in cities and communities across Canada from Saint John, New Brunswick, to Galiano, British Columbia. The Ottawa community loan fund was one of the first to be established.[14] These loan funds recruit investment and donations from community members and then provide accessible financing to fuel innovation, expand opportunities and improve lives in the community.

Social Enterprise Development in Europe

Although social enterprises, albeit under different names, had been around in Europe for some time, they took on a more significant role in the early 1990s as European governments started to develop special legislation to accommodate social enterprises. Italy for one has been a pioneer in this regard by introducing in 1991 a new legal form referred to as "social cooperative." There are two possible forms of this multi stakeholder co-op. Type A brings together producers and beneficiaries of a social service as members, while Type B brings together permanent workers and previously unemployed people who wish to integrate into the labour market. By 2005, there were 7300 such social enterprises in Italy employing 244,000 workers.[15] Other European countries followed suit although the names given to these initiatives vary.

In the United Kingdom, the government unveiled an innovative social enterprise strategy in 2002 with a dedicated government unit and provided funding for the Social Enterprise Coalition, an organization to support social enterprises. It adopted a contrasting definition of social enterprise, one that minimizes issues related to structure and participation and insists only on the delivery of social benefits and limited distribution of profits. In 2004 the U.K. passed legislation referring to social enterprises as community interest companies (CIC), and by 2005 there were 15,000 companies registered as CIC. The U.K. approach is pragmatic and focuses on social outcomes rather than legal structure (for-profit or not-for-profit).[16]

Real Goods for Real Customers

Social enterprises come in a variety of shapes and forms. One of the strengths of the social economy and social enterprise movement is the ability to shape such organizations to meet the needs of local communities. While not well developed in Canada, social enterprises are gaining momentum, in part because of the failure of conventional corporations to meet the needs of people. Yet, for all their diversity (whether co-ops, for-profit or not-for-profit corporations), social enterprises share a common heritage, ideology and vision: economic organizations can and must work towards social justice goals at the same time as striving for and achieving "revenue surplus" goals.

To achieve their dual (social and economic) goals, social enterprises will continue for the foreseeable future to rely on various forms of funding, particularly for start-up. But, those public and private "subsidies" and various forms of "patient capital" will be rewarded with successful alternative economic development, especially once there is a critical mass of social enterprises in Canada. But if there is one lesson to be learned by the social enterprise experience to date, it is this: although social enterprises incorporate and pursue a social mission, they rely on earned income from sales to customers and in competition with private sector enterprises.

Notes

1. Borzaga and Defourny 2001.
2. Chantier de l'economie sociale 2008.
3. Quarter, Mook and Armstrong 2009.
4. The term profit is used with for-profit enterprises and is associated with a tax liability, whereas the term surplus is used in relation to not-for-profit organizations and it has no tax liability associated with it.
5. Borzaga and Defourny 2001.
6. <http://www.secouncil.ca/en/general-information-other/about-social-enterprise>.
7. <http://www.se-alliance.org/>.
8. <http://www.socialenterprise.org.uk/>.
9. <http://www.emes.net>.
10. The position by Revenue Canada on this type of transfer from a for-profit corporation to a not-for-profit charity shareholder is ambiguous and seems to depend on the relationship between the two organizations and their social mission.
11. Loughheed and Donkervoort 2009.
12. Kardash and Mochoruk 2000.
13. O'Connor et al. 2012.
14. <www.oclf.org/>.
15. Gonzales 2010.
16. Defourny and Nyssen 2008.

Chapter 8

Outcomes and Learnings

By most measures, ICR is a successful social enterprise. That it survived its first decade and is now flourishing is in itself testimony that we did something right. While there have been setbacks and lessons learned, ICR has stuck to its social mission and its belief in the need to provide real goods for real customers in order to successfully sustain itself.

Over my ten-year tenure, ICR provided 125 good jobs — well paid with benefits and training. For those who stayed for a minimum amount of time, those good jobs were the basis of changed lives, economically, socially and personally. We did find out, not really to our surprise, that there would be as many employee failures as successes; our turnover rate was around 50 percent, and several employees returned to gang life. And, the employee successes require diligence and patience. The ICR commitment to hard-to-employ people means always "going the extra mile" — in training, personal issue support, setting up bank accounts and so on — but, in the end it pays off for both employees and for ICR.

Similarly, ICR plays an important community role in the North End. Providing good jobs and building affordable housing means that ICR is giving to, not taking from, this very poor inner city community. While it cannot solve the problems of the North End, it does contribute to making life better for North End residents. To do that, ICR has to be economically successful, and it took eight years to achieve that goal, which for ICR is profitability and 95 percent earned revenue. We learned that economic success for a social enterprise includes following some fairly standard business practices: having a solid plan to start with, sticking to the plan, staying within capacities in the early years, having some committed and patient start-up funds, having solid technical skills in the organization and so on. We learned that a social enterprise has to accept lower productivity because of its social justice commitment, but lower productivity only means lower profit rather than no profit.

Employee-Related Outcomes

Twelve inner city residents, previously unemployed and on social assistance, obtained full-time jobs in ICR's start-up year. This number gradually increased to approximately thirty people working at permanent, full-time jobs by year three. Wages are equal to or better than average in the renovation construction sector. All employees as well as their families receive extended health and dental benefits paid for by the company. Employees and their families receive a range of social supports provided by a social worker. The company also arranges social activities, which provide a sense of connectedness and well-being. Employees are able to obtain better housing and nutrition both from their earnings and assistance from the social worker. New employees to the construction sector are provided with basic tools and safety equipment as well as on-the-job training by skilled and experienced journeypersons. Employees are treated with respect and gain dignity. Since ICR established itself, there has been a steady stream of applicants seeking employment with ICR.

In year four (2006), ICR assisted employees to set up bank accounts and implemented automatic payroll deposit. Most of the employees had been cashing their paycheques at the local branches of cheque cashing and payroll loan companies, a service for which employees paid dearly. Having bank accounts not only saves employees money but also makes it easier and safer to deal with cash. At around the same time, ICR expanded the employee benefit plan to include long-term disability (LTD) coverage. The cost of the LTD is borne by the employees so that potential benefits will be tax-free.

ICR assists employees with apprenticeship training. In the first eight years, ten employees were enrolled in the provincial apprenticeship program and one graduated from the program as a journey carpenter. ICR raises employees' wage levels on an annual basis. In 2007, ICR set up a trial savings program providing two dollars for every one dollar paid into the plan by the employee up to a set limit. Although some employees were able to take advantage of the incentive, most did not as they needed their entire pay to cover daily expenses.

Over the years, several Aboriginal employees of ICR have been recognized for their positive life changes. These events are celebrated with ceremonies led by Aboriginal elders.

As ICR entered its mature stage, many of the employees who started with ICR in its early years were able to stabilize their lives. Some other long-term employees, however, continue to live chaotic lives, coping with various life struggles from one pay period to the next despite the supports provided by ICR. Employment alone, even with its social supports, is not always sufficient to deal with ongoing health issues and addictions and to alter lifelong learned behaviour and patterns. For those employees who only worked at ICR for a short period, the ICR experience was but a pit stop on their life journey, and they were unable to take full advantage of the opportunity and went back to gang culture, homelessness or (for the more fortunate ones) social welfare assistance. Given the recruitment process, this result is not unexpected. Opportunity and supports are not necessarily sufficient to affect permanent change in all of ICR's employees. People have to be willing and open to take personal responsibility to change their lives around.

Overall, full-time, year-round work with higher wages allows employees to obtain better housing and improve their quality of life. Some are able to get their children out of institutional care, while others are able to care for their extended families. Those employees leaving ICR leave with marketable skills, which provide access to new employment opportunities. Between 2002 and 2010, approximately a dozen workers moved directly from ICR to other construction jobs. Others benefit from the training and experience gained while working at ICR at some later point in their lives. As is often the case, tracking employees after they have left a company can be difficult, and ICR's experience is no different.

Diversity

In keeping with ICR's mandate to create employment for inner city residents, its workforce reflects the demographics and diversity of the community. More than 50 percent of all employees throughout the eight-year period of 2002–2010, were Aboriginal. Although most of ICR employees are men, there are a number of women apprentices. Ages range from early twenties to mid fifties; however, most of the employees are in their late thirties or early forties. Employees include single individuals and single parents as well as parents with large families with many dependents. The common thread among the employees is that they come from a low-income situation and an inner city location. This diversity in sex, age and culture brings people together so that they can learn from each other. Unlike workplaces providing training intended specifically for youth, women, immigrants or Aboriginal people, ICR's experience was not to segregate into these groups. Diversity at ICR avoids tokenism by having more than one or two representatives from each demographic. Not being the only woman, young person or minority creates a more comfortable and accepting environment. Diversity is not limited to crew employees. Senior and middle management includes both age and sex diversity but falls short on cultural diversity. There is no question that the cultural, age and sex diversity among ICR's employees contributes to ICR's overall success.

Success Rates

ICR started up with a total of thirteen employees: ten crewmembers, one supervisor and two management staff. Of the original crewmembers, three were still with ICR at 2010 year-end, two had died and two moved to other provinces (B.C. and Ontario), two transitioned to other companies in the construction sector, one went on health related social benefits, and one cannot be traced.

Over the eight-year period between August 1, 2002, and July 31, 2010, ICR employed a total of 125 different people. As the average number of employees at any one time was twenty-five, ICR experienced quite a high turnover rate, approaching 50 percent. It is difficult to compare this turnover rate to an industry average in the construction sector as many workers move from one employer or project to another and are not full-time employees of a specific company. Employees leave ICR for many different reasons: some leave to take on employment with other companies in the construction sector and others leave for employment in other sectors; still others leave employment for personal reasons, including health or family issues.

Due to the transient nature of the workforce, tracking employees after they leave ICR is very difficult. ICR has lost track of more than half of the departing employees. Some of those no doubt returned to their previous life circumstances, including social welfare or a gang. A review of the personal outcomes of forty-eight employees who are no longer employed by ICR revealed that twenty-eight left for work with, and remain employed at, other companies in the construction sector, six left the construction sector to work elsewhere, four returned to their First Nation communities for personal reasons, five left for health related reasons, including addictions, and five died while employed by ICR. Considering the life circumstances of many employees when they started with ICR, this is a relatively good outcome. Regardless of the length of time spent working at ICR, most employees have a positive experience, learning new skills and getting social support.

One of the most important learnings from ICR's experience is that given an appropriate and supportive environment, people previously outside of the traditional labour market can become productive participants in the economy. Just as importantly, they can obtain a sense of personal well-being, pride, respect and dignity. The projects completed by ICR over the years are a testimonial to the skills and commitment of its workers.

Community-Related Outcomes

ICR has established itself as an integral part of the local community. Its early relationships with community social housing developers provided ICR with its initial income as well as recognition in the community. ICR also developed relationships with local suppliers and sub contractors. This was important initially as these companies and others in the community had no experience with social enterprises and were skeptical and unsure about ICR's sustainability.

ICR plays an important role in providing affordable and safe social housing in the community. It helped turn the tide in the decline of the housing infrastructure in the city's North End and started addressing the renewal of commercial properties.

ICR has become entrenched in the community both as an employer providing local jobs and as a contractor committed to working for the betterment of the community. Both government agencies and non-government organizations (NGOs) have reached out to support ICR's work in the community. As ICR became successful, it began assisting other community organizations interested in developing social enterprises. ICR often gives presentations on its development and success to organizations across Canada.

ICR employees are role models in the community, role models for transforming people's lives. Some leave gang life behind while others start a new life after coming out of prison. Some with mental health challenges are able to work for the first time and feel positive about their contribution. ICR has improved the skill set of several inner city residents and has created a small pool of trained and skilled people. In a minor way, ICR, with its high percentage of Aboriginal employees, paves the foundation for improved relationships between Aboriginal and non-Aboriginal communities. ICR's Aboriginal employees demonstrate their skill and determination to others in the community.

ICR not only provides income and training to its employees but it deliberately recruits people from disenfranchised parts of the community. ICR pursues and offers positions to people coming out of jail and those trying to leave gangs, as well as people coping with mental health or addiction issues. The failure to reintegrate those who have gone through the criminal justice system has a negative effect on everyone in the community. By going to job fairs at local prisons and offering hope and opportunity to those trying to reintegrate into the community, ICR provides an essential service for the betterment of all. Employing people and providing supports to those with mental health or addiction issues is another way of creating a more equal society. Giving individuals a chance or in some cases a second chance is critical to creating a more equal, safer and better community for all its members.

The city core, and particularly the North End of Winnipeg, experiences numerous social problems associated with poverty, not the least of which are relatively high unemployment rates. At the same time, there is a growing need for skilled construction workers both in Winnipeg and elsewhere. A strategy to deal with both of these realities is to recruit individuals from the inner city, including members from the Aboriginal community and provide training and supports to increase the long-term viability of this strategy. This includes sensitivity to both Aboriginal culture and issues related to people coming from institutional and systemic poverty. By recruiting people from these sectors and providing necessary supports, ICR in a small but significant way sustains a measure of equality at the local community level.

Company-Related Outcomes

ICR has established itself as a credible enterprise in the construction sector. It negotiated office and warehouse space, purchased a truck and the necessary tools and equipment. It negotiated and set up an essential line of credit with a financial institution. It built on its relationships in the residential sector.

With its success in the residential social housing sector, ICR diversified its services and entered the commercial and institutional market. It completed numerous projects on Selkirk Avenue in Winnipeg's North End as well as in other parts of the city. ICR as a subcontractor successfully built two new branches for Assiniboine Credit Union. It renovated daycares, senior residences, health centres and other buildings for community organizations.

ICR also developed relationships with architects and designers, resulting from working with them on a number of significant projects. The entry into the commercial sector, in addition to the private residential sector, resulted in higher profit margins. By 2009, ICR had become profitable and had eliminated its accumulated deficit. Throughout the years, ICR received grant income to support its social mission, especially its training component. The earned revenue from operations went from 70 percent in 2003 to 96 percent in 2010. Earned revenue went from $936,000 in the first year to $1.7 million in 2010. This compares very favourably with other social enterprises in Canada, whose earned revenue accounts for 40–60 percent on average. At 96 percent or better, it even compares favourably to private sector enterprises that also receive grants and government incentives.

Over time ICR started to receive recognition for its role and its achievements. In 2008, the Manitoba Provincial Apprentice Board chose ICR as the Provincial Employer of the Year covering all trades. The following year, ICR won a provincial sustainability award. See Appendix 3 for a complete list of awards.

ICR is positioned for future expansion and success. It has a trained and stable workforce, countless satisfied customers providing testimonials and more than a hundred completed projects, including some high profile ones well recognized around the city. It has beneficial relationships with subcontractors and architects and memberships in the Better Business Bureau and the local homebuilders association. Perhaps most important of all, ICR has developed partnerships and mutual relationships with community organizations, including those in the Aboriginal community.

Business-Related Outcomes/Learnings

As in any business, ICR has gone through the various stages of the business life cycle: pre start-up, start-up, growth, expansion and mature phase. There were learnings and outcomes in each of these developmental stages.

Pre Start-up Phase

In this phase, potential enterprise opportunities were identified, analyzed and prioritized. It was important not to rush this phase, as it can be a critical period for the future success of an enterprise. Ideally, we were looking for an opportunity where there was an unfulfilled demand and few or no barriers to entry into the sector. In ICR's case, job creation, good wages and training opportunities were key criteria in its search for such a community need (market) opportunity.

A feasibility analysis was conducted on each potential opportunity. Once feasibility had been established on a business idea for the social enterprise, a thorough business plan was developed. Both income and cash flow projections ought to be conservative. Revenue is often less than projected and expenses tend to be higher; the combination can be critical to the early success or failure of the enterprise.

It was very important to make sure there were sufficient financial resources in place for the start-up period. It is much more difficult to access financing once the enterprise has started up. Financial institutions are particularly reluctant to finance cash flow difficulties where the enterprise has insufficient funds to cover its payables within a timely fashion. It was also during this pre start-up period that a network of supportive individuals and organizations was developed. As was the case with ICR, it had secured contracts before its start-up to make sure it had work and income once it opened its doors. Being able to show that the enterprise had committed contracts made it much easier to secure loans and open up line of credit with a financial institution.

Start-up Phase

It is important to stick to the business plan during the start-up phase. It can be tempting to go off in different directions to pursue other opportunities that come up during this phase. Although the business plan is a living document that should be adapted and revised as the enterprise develops, it requires a time to develop before changing course. It is also important to walk before running. As a business, a social enterprise must not take on more than it can handle, especially in its early years. ICR learned this the hard way in taking on a major commercial project in the latter part of its first year. It did not have the necessary resources and although it satisfactorily completed the project, it lost a significant amount of money in the process. It was a costly experience, one that could have put the company out of business if it wasn't for access to additional funding from its shareholders.

It is also critical to provide effective leadership during this start-up phase. Employees need confidence in the leadership of the enterprise. Leading by example was a wonderful management strategy. During ICR's start-up phase, I allocated one day a month to work as a crewmember on construction sites alongside other workers under the direction of the crew supervisor. This not only provided a positive impression with the employees but also gave me insight into on-site issues that I otherwise might not be aware of.

One of the few things a social enterprise can offer right from the beginning is a respectful workplace. Management can set an example by treating its employees with dignity and encouraging employees to treat each other the same way. A code of conduct has to be established and communicated to all employees along with consequences for violating the code.

As the goal of many social enterprises, including ICR, is to create employment for its target group, there is a temptation to take on too many novices and not enough skilled personnel. Again ICR was guilty of this temptation and had to readjust the ratio of non-skilled to skilled workers during this start-up period. It ended up with a ratio of no more than 3:1 (unskilled to skilled), which was manageable.

During the start-up phase, ICR management was spending too much time dealing with its employees' personal issues and problems. This took both time and focus away from the task of managing the business. It was during this phase that ICR contracted a social worker on a part-time basis to deal with employees' personal issues, especially as they affected their ability to perform their tasks. The social worker, Larry Morrissette, also arranged and managed social functions, including traditional sweats and other Aboriginal ceremonies as well as sport and leisure activities.

Growth Phase

One of the key learnings during this phase was how to address and improve productivity. During the start-up phase, training accounted for 20 percent of the total labour costs. Productivity therefore was estimated at only 80 percent of what a fully trained and skilled workforce would produce. This was in part due to training unskilled workers, but it was also related to unproductive time such as late starts, extended breaks and stopping work early. Finding the right balance between having a supportive/pleasant and productive workplace can be difficult. It is difficult to tighten up rules once employees get used to a more relaxed atmosphere. Unfortunately, it is very difficult to enforce strict rules when transitioning people into gainful employment for the first time. Although ICR's social worker, Larry Morrissette, assisted employees with this transition and coping with the realities of full-time work and thereby reducing the productivity gap, ICR was unable to eliminate the productivity gap all together during this period.

Although at the outset ICR was fortunate to have 100 percent of its work provided by its community housing developer partners, it became a liability during this phase for a couple of reasons. As with any enterprise depending on only one or two customers, ICR was completely dependent on contracts from these organizations. In addition, renovation projects from these partners came in spurts, leaving ICR with insufficient work at times. More importantly, the margins associated with this work were too small, often insufficient to cover ICR's overhead, never mind making a contribution to profit. The most important of these reasons was ICR's dependence on its shareholder partners, leaving it in a very vulnerable position should anything happen to them. This actually came to pass as one shareholder ran out of eligible properties to renovate, one choose to once again deal with traditional contractors and another, the North End Housing Project, responsible for more than a million dollars of ICR's annual revenue, ceased operations. These events necessitated a change to the original business plan. ICR started pursuing more projects in the commercial sector as well as in the private residential sector. Therefore, a social enterprise may have to diversify its customer base, resulting in both less dependence on any one sector, higher profit margins and continuity of available work.

Contrary to early beliefs that most people will support a social enterprise like ICR because of its social mission, I learned during this phase that this is not necessarily the case. In fact, the contrary is true. Confronted with having work done by a social enterprise, most potential customers assume that it is more expensive, lower quality and less dependable. This experience has been verified by other successful social enterprises with hiring practices similar to those of ICR. Potluck Catering, located in Vancouver's Downtown East Side, employs people from their community and has received the same kind of feedback as ICR.[1] The learning is to market the enterprise on quality, dependable service and competitive pricing. Use the social mission only with customers who you know are supportive of this aspect of the enterprise.

Another key learning during this phase was patience, related both to reaching financial break-even and to fulfilling the social objectives. ICR did not break-even until year five and that still included grant income although to a lesser extent than in previous years. The original business plan had projected break-even much sooner, possibly year two and definitely by year three. It required patience and ongoing commitment to stay the course and continue. On the social side, although ICR was able to deliver on many of its social goals early on — e.g., employment, wages and benefits and training — there was an expectation on my part that employment at ICR would have more significant impacts on people's lives. With the passing years, it became evident that my expectations were too ambitious. Significant and lasting impacts may take more than one generation as the current generation sets an example for the next. Working parents become role models for their children. Meaningful work and related income become the new norm instead of dependence on welfare or income from criminal activity. I had to readjust my expectations related to timeframe for real social change.

Training was another learning exercise during this phase. ICR was committed to encouraging its employees to pursue not just on-the-job training but enrolment in the provincial apprenticeship program. Although some employees were able to manage this formal training, completing certain levels of the four year program, and a couple went through the entire program to obtain their journeyperson credentials, many were not able to cope. Lack of minimal academic standing was a barrier to entry for some, while for others the formal nature of classroom training was not appropriate. ICR tried to provide academic upgrading, tutors and mentors but to no avail. The learning from this experience was that on-the-job training works best for many in the target employee group.

The potential for employee ownership was one of the aspirations in setting up ICR. It was one of the reasons for its legal structure (share capital corporation), which made it possible for employees to own shares in the enterprise. Ownership discussions with employees throughout this growth phase revealed that this was not a priority for them. Many are more concerned about their short-term income and their personal issues than taking on the responsibility and risk associated with ownership in the enterprise. In addition, individual ownership is not a significant issue in Aboriginal culture, which is more concerned about community ownership and sharing. The learning therefore is not to presume what is best or appropriate for others.

Expansion Phase

During the expansion phase in 2006, ICR started up two new social enterprises: Inner City Janitorial (ICJ) and Inner City Property Management (ICPM), which were both subsequently shutdown as they were unable to reach the necessary economies of scale for sustainability. Some key learnings from this expansion into related but new areas include the danger of making invalid assumptions in the research during the feasibility phase.

One of the key failures related to the janitorial enterprise was to assume that minimum wage legislation applied to all businesses in this sector. Additional research would have revealed that in fact most workers in this sector are self-employed contract workers paid on a piece work basis and thus that minimum wage legislation does not apply. Another lesson was related to supervision and backup, as there is no tolerance for workers not showing up for their shift. Buildings and facilities need to be cleaned nightly. There has to be proper supervision and backup plans to make sure that all contracts are fulfilled on a daily basis. All of these issues should have been discovered and analyzed during the feasibility stage. Sometimes, as this example shows, assumptions are made without verification and other issues are missed completely.

The ICPM venture ran into problems related mainly to the financial realities and constraints of their clients. As the economy took a downturn, affecting among other things government and charitable organization grants, ICPM's clients, which were all non-profit community organizations, were forced to re-evaluate their budgets and programs. One of the consequences of these cutbacks for ICPM was clients cutting out the 5 percent fee for property management services and having their own existing staff perform this service.

Mature Phase

By the end of year eight, ICR was on the cusp of entering the mature phase of its life cycle. It is still early in this phase to identify related learnings but there are some.

One such lesson is to stick with what is working. You can adjust the business model based on experiences gained over the years and adapt to new opportunities and threats in the environment. In ICR's case, it learned that individual fixed price projects in excess of a million dollars expose the enterprise to excessive risk. Large fixed price contracts always carry a higher risk due to the amount of money involved and more significant implications if a mistake is made. This kind of project had not been contemplated in the original business model at ICR's start-up. Taking on the Urban Circle project in ICR's mature stage would still have carried some risk, but ICR would have fared better due to more experience in preparing quotes and access to a better trained and experienced workforce.

Meeting tight deadlines that require longer hours or additional resources can also present difficulties, resulting in cost overruns and/or penalties for not completing a project on time. Although presented with various opportunities to pursue projects out of Winnipeg, ICR turned them down due to various logistical problems, not the least of which was the unwillingness of the employees to travel and be away from their families for periods of time.

Dependence on unearned revenue in the form of grants from government or charities can present a danger as they can expire or be withdrawn. In its early start-up years, ICR was dependent on this kind of funding, as it represented as much as 30 percent of the revenue necessary for break-even. Anxious about being dependent on grant funding for its survival, ICR gradually increased earned revenue to account for more than 95 percent in year eight. Becoming financially independent is a key objective for the sustainability of a social enterprise.

Note

1.   Loughheed and Donkervoort 2009.

Chapter 9

Challenges and Opportunities

Much can be learned about the challenges facing a social enterprise, as well as the opportunities available to it, from ICR's experience competing with private sector enterprises in the marketplace. Perhaps surprisingly, it is not always clear whether an issue is a challenge or an opportunity. Often they go together, as an opportunity can also present a challenge and a challenge can present an opportunity. Our challenges and opportunities are/were not unique to ICR; they present important lessons for other social enterprises. The ICR experience cannot be copied precisely in other markets or in other communities, but neither do new social enterprises need to learn the hard way, as we did. There are elements of ICR that stand the test of time: in general, that achieving social justice goals in an economic organization requires acting like a real business. In the larger picture, ICR, as illustrative of a successful social enterprise, clearly demonstrates that there are alternative social, economic and political approaches to a capitalist economic approach that is failing so many of us.

Challenges

There are numerous challenges in starting any enterprise, including access to capital, finding competent and committed staff, and generating sales and income to become profitable. Social enterprises face these and many more challenges.

Although there were a few social enterprises, like Versatech Industries Inc. (now ImagineAbility Inc.) and Neechi Foods Co-op Ltd., established before ICR's start-up in 2002, there was a general lack of awareness and understanding of social enterprises in the Manitoba economy, as in all of Canada and many other countries. ICR not only faced all of the usual obstacles for a new enterprise but was challenged to do so with an unskilled and untested labour pool. These challenges were perceived to be insurmountable even by some of ICR's adamant supporters. ICR not only survived but grew over the next decade to become self-sustaining. Although awareness of and supports for social enterprises have increased in recent years, social enterprises still face some of the same challenges ICR experienced through its first few years.

Social-Business Balance

There are a number of difficult issues for social enterprises related to achieving their social goals, which is the main reason for setting up the enterprise. These goals are either pursued directly as part of the social enterprise or

103

indirectly as an earned revenue strategy to support the social goals of the parent not-for-profit community organization. Social goals vary and range from employment creation for specific target groups or delivery of a specific product or service for the betterment of the community. Whatever the social goals, they can only be achieved if the enterprise is financially sustainable. Therefore, there has to be a balance between social and financial goals. Therein lies the challenge, as these goals are not complementary but can work against each other. This tension is exacerbated since achieving the social goals is the driving force behind the creation of the enterprise. There is often a cost related to achieving the social goal, which negatively affects the financial sustainability of the enterprise. This, together with the fact that social enterprises are often managed by people with social work/social justice training can create a bias towards achieving the enterprise's social goals at the expense of the financial goals. On the other hand, managers trained in traditional business concepts and practice can lean towards putting the enterprise's financial goals first. This delicate balance can shift over time as the enterprise becomes established.

Business

One of the biggest challenges facing social enterprises is to compete as a business with other businesses in the marketplace. The enterprise needs to find and establish a competitive advantage. A social enterprise cannot rely on its social mission as its main advantage in establishing itself in the market.

The initial challenge is to find a business model that not only fulfills the social goals but also responds to a need for a product or service in the market. After coming up with numerous ideas and conducting several feasibility studies on promising concepts, ICR found such an opportunity in the construction sector, focusing on social housing in the North End of Winnipeg. All too often, social enterprises try to start up in a crowded inhospitable market where they have no competitive advantage beyond trying to capitalize on their social goals. ICR, however, found a niche that responded to a need in the market, which gave it the ability to offer fair wages and benefits, skill training and, due to the potential size of the enterprise, opportunities for advancement.

Access to capital is a significant difficulty for most social enterprise start-ups. ICR was fortunate to have two shareholders, Community Ownership Solutions and Social Capital Partners, which were able to provide start-up funding and cover initial operational losses. ICR was also fortunate to have a supportive lender in Assiniboine Credit Union, which supplied both loans for capital acquisition and a line of credit to support cash flow. The legal structure, especially in a not-for-profit model, can create barriers to traditional financing from mainstream banks. This has been mitigated to some extent by the establishment of community loan funds to support investing in the community, including in social enterprises.[1] It is imperative that social enterprises have access to various forms of capital, including grants, loans and equity. Both grants and loans were critical to ICR's start-up.

Management

One of the biggest challenges facing social enterprises is finding appropriate management staff. Social enterprise managers must have technical and business competence, passion for social equity and justice, and above all, be sensitive human relations leaders. Based on his experience with social enterprises, Bill Young, of Social Capital Partners, indicated that "running a social enterprise is among the most challenging jobs in the economy. To do this job well one must have all the business skills and dedication of a private sector entrepreneur combined with the patience and emotional IQ of a social worker."[2]

This lesson was learned the hard way in ICR's initial years. The first crop of general managers at ICR had construction industry technical qualifications, some business management skills and very little in the way of the social leadership skills, which are critical to a social enterprise. Consequently, ICR had three general managers in its first four years. None of them provided the complete skill set necessary for successfully managing a social enterprise. The COS board ultimately decided to redirect its resources in an all or bust decision to second its general manager, putting me into the ICR general manager position. Although I lacked technical construction skills and experience, I had the necessary business training and experience as well as a passion for the social mission. During the first five years of the enterprise, I had earned the respect of the employees, and I was able to provide the leadership necessary to sustain the enterprise and lead it to a profitable position without sacrificing any part of the social mission. Ideally a social enterprise manager should possess all of these qualities and skills; however, this is often next to impossible.

Based on my experience managing ICR, I would place more emphasis on business management skills than technical skills related to the enterprise. The necessary technical skills, such as construction experience in ICR's case, can be obtained via other middle management positions. However, social justice passion and leadership traits cannot be compromised and are critical to the success of the enterprise.

Until recently, social enterprise was not a topic covered at business schools. Graduates tended to follow traditional paths to private for-profit enterprises or to start their own business with the expectation of creating personal wealth. The developing attraction of students to social enterprise is a reflection of their interest in meaningful work that includes social and environmental issues as well as careers that go beyond maximizing personal income. This reality is slowly changing curriculums at business schools to include social enterprise. Programs in social work, community economic development and urban and inner city studies are also interested in this topic, and some are starting to include social enterprise related courses.

In addition to finding qualified senior management, the enterprise must also find appropriate people for middle management positions. ICR was fortunate to attract Cheryl Lisoway as its office manager. She had both construction sector management experience and sympathies for ICR's social mission. She began work at ICR prior to its start-up and is still with ICR, having taken on additional management responsibilities. ICR has been less fortunate in its project manager positions. Most of the people in this position had the technical construction expertise but lacked commitment for the mission. Some became educated about the social mission and started to be passionate about it after a while. It is not always possible to get project managers with both technical expertise and passion for the social mission. For some sectors, like construction, it is critical to have the technical capability; passion for the social mission must be secondary. ICR went through numerous project managers when finally in year eight, it found a competent and committed person for the job. Attracting skilled and committed crew supervisors was less of a problem, and ICR has been fortunate to attracting some competent and passionate individuals.

Another difficulty for a social enterprise is to attract individuals to its board of directors. In addition to supporting the enterprise's social mission, directors should bring a mixture of relevant business and technical skills. Although ICR has been fortunate in this regard, it has been unsuccessful in attracting board members with specific construction sector knowledge and experience. Either these people were too busy, perceived to be in a conflict situation as potential competitors or just did not buy into the social enterprise concept. This is an important issue for social enterprises in general as they struggle to find willing, passionate and business minded directors.

Staffing

Recruiting staff from the target group can also be difficult, especially for social enterprises committed to creating employment opportunities for the hard to employ. There are always more people interested in being hired than there are available positions. It is hard to decide who to hire and who not to hire, especially as all are deserving and in need of a job. Most of the ICR recruiting was done through a community employment agency, which screened candidates for work readiness, looking for such attributes as relatively stable environment, no current addictions and willingness to work. This relationship worked well for ICR and is recommended for other social enterprises dealing with job creation with a marginalized target group.

Finding the right balance between unskilled target employees and more skilled employees can also represent a significant challenge. The tendency is to try to provide too many jobs that require training for those in the unskilled target group, as this is the key desired social outcome. Yet, to develop into a self-sustaining organization, a social enterprise needs to maintain a relatively skilled workforce in order to compete in the market against private sector companies. It has to provide a dependable service or a quality product at a competitive price. Too many unskilled workers can easily compromise the enterprise's ability to compete effectively. In its early years, ICR found itself in the position of having too many unskilled workers on its crews and had to take the corrective action of reducing the ratio of trainees to skilled supervisors. It may be best to err on the side of caution in the beginning. Once a social enterprise is established and has a larger skilled contingent, the ratio may be adjusted as trainees learn from other workers not just supervisors.

Many social enterprises include skill training as one of their social objectives. ICR falls into this category. Providing skill training to individuals that have not completed high school and in some cases have great difficulty reading presents a significant challenge to their training goals. The Manitoba Apprenticeship and Certification Board, for example, requires candidates to have successfully completed grade 12, with exceptions for some demographic groups to completion of grade 10 English and mathematics. A number of ICR's employees needed academic upgrading in order to gain entrance to the apprenticeship program. For adults with little schooling to start with and who have been out of school for a long time, academic learning can be very difficult. ICR tried by providing classroom instruction, small private tutoring and even one-on-one mentoring and still failed to get any of these employees to the necessary entrance level. On-the-job, hands-on training by skilled supervisors and peers was much more successful but did not provide the official accreditation, useful should they move to other employers. Private sector capitalist corporations tend to be hesitant to provide academic upgrading necessary to enroll workers in professional development programs. These training related challenges have an impact on productivity and the ability for a social enterprise to compete in the market.

Reaching the productivity level necessary to compete with private for-profit enterprises in the market can also be a challenge. Many factors related to some workforces in social enterprises make this difficult. It may take more patience and understanding to train a social enterprise workforce. The inclusion of totally unskilled workers reduces productivity. It takes time for employees to become fully productive as they learn the necessary skills and adapt to full-time work. In addition, training takes time away from skilled supervisors, decreasing their productivity, as they can often spend up to 20 percent of their time training and supervising unskilled workers. Although some private sector construction companies support workers with training, given the choice, they would probably hire a skilled person rather than an unskilled one. These companies often hire unskilled casual labour for some of the grunt work without any commitment to train them for more skilled positions.

Other factors besides training affect productivity. Work habits such as showing up ready to commence work on time, limiting coffee and lunch breaks to set times and working until the end of the workday are important. Absenteeism is also a significant factor affecting productivity as workers deal with childcare and other family related issues, health issues and parole officers. At ICR, absenteeism increased the first workday after payday. In private sector enterprises these issues are usually dealt with by dismissal. At ICR, as in all employment-related social enterprises, this behaviour, while not condoned, was accepted as part of its social mandate. Some social enterprises, like ICR, engage a social worker to assist employees with personal issues affecting their work habits. With supports as well time and patience, these issues can be resolved without dismissal.

ICR's commitment to participative management also affected productivity. Although ICR had a quarterly staff newsletter to communicate performance issues, upcoming projects and social events, it also convened regular monthly staff meetings. These were always held during paid working hours to ensure attendance. Workers often gave up their lunch break as part of their commitment to the process and the enterprise provided lunch. In addition to these staff meetings, there were also supervisor meetings, safety meetings and social-committee meetings, all during working hours. This approach to participative management is not necessarily adopted by all social enterprises.

Marketing

Marketing a social enterprise's products or services can be an extremely daunting process. Depending on social justice values of potential customers, a call to support the enterprise's social goals is not sufficient and can actually be a liability. Upon learning about the enterprise's social component, potential customers often assume inferior quality, undependable service and non-competitive pricing for the product or service. Similar to private sector enterprises, marketing must be based on quality work, dependable service and competitive pricing; in these areas a social enterprise has to engage with mainstream business practices. ICR learned this the hard way, as work from expected customers did not materialize. In my discussions with other social enterprises across the country, ICR's experience was confirmed. ICR subsequently marketed its services based on quality, dependability and competitive pricing and added the information about the social cause only with receptive potential customers.

Successful marketing is often based on having a competitive advantage.

ICR had such a competitive advantage based on its relationship with its four initial shareholders, which provided an order file in excess of a million dollars at start-up. This commitment and relationship provided ICR with time to develop other customers. Partnering with potential purchasers of the enterprise's product or service is an excellent strategy to start up a social enterprise.

Business Sustainability

Since social enterprises are by and large still newcomers to the main economy, it is critical to avoid failures, especially in high profile social enterprises. Like any other start-up enterprise, there is a very high risk of failure in the first year. According to Industry Canada, about 15 percent of all businesses that started up in 2005 failed in the first year. This number increased to 49 percent failure at the five-year mark.[3] Unfortunately, failures in a developing sector, especially in one where there is some skepticism, can be harmful to the overall development of the sector. Avoiding high profile failures is a major challenge for the social enterprise sector. It may mean being more selective in new start-ups as well as publicizing the successes.

The social objectives of social enterprises, such as training, accommodating people with disabilities and providing social supports have an associated cost. This cost is in part related to lower productivity and in part to out-of-pocket expenses for "social programs." The question then becomes: Can the enterprise reach sufficient scale and profitability to pay for all of these related expenses? In ICR's case, the enterprise required annual grants to support its social agenda. Once ICR had 95 percent of its income based on earned revenue and only 5 percent from grants, it was able to sustain itself. This ratio of earned income to grant income to sustain a social enterprise will vary from one social enterprise to another depending on the sector, the stage in its life cycle and the scope of its social agenda.

Bill Young, president of Social Capital Partners and shareholder in ICR, identified five critical factors related to the profitability of a social enterprise.[4] Two factors, the inherent business capacity of the social enterprise and the complexity of the business, are referred to as the business factors, as they only affect the financial bottom line. The other three are referred to as trade-off factors because of the relationship between social and financial performance. These include the size and complexity of employment barriers of the employees, the skills and training gap, and the degree of emphasis on the social mission in the day-to-day operations. The five factors together impact the profitability and sustainability of a social enterprise. Young's analysis of these factors was in part based on SCP's experience with ICR.

Politics

Governments have a role and some would say a duty to provide social programs related to education, training, health and childcare. The current trend of neoliberal and conservative governments is to privatize the delivery of many government services, including social programs. Some people fear that these governments may see an opportunity to offload some of their social service responsibilities to social enterprises as part of governments' privatization and deficit cutting strategies. This raises the danger of social enterprises being co-opted, since these governments have not accepted nor supported the real goals of social enterprise in the economy. One of the reasons for the recent developing role of social enterprises in countries around the world is related to the support received from social democrat and labour governments. Should these governments be replaced with more conservative ones, the role of social enterprises may be in jeopardy.

Social enterprises need to be on guard against government offloading of social services and to recognize real commitment to the role of social enterprises in the economy versus a role in the privatization of social services. The overarching challenge is to become more financially independent so as not to be beholden to government.

Many of us advocating for and creating social enterprises are fearful that we are feeding into this privatization and offloading paradigm. The practice of governments offloading services to social enterprises can be a slippery slope, similar to what happened with food banks, which have become an integral part of feeding the poor.

Opportunities

Despite these considerable challenges facing social enterprises there are also opportunities. Social enterprises have certain advantages that can lead to and provide opportunities.

The Local Economy

Similar to the popularity of the slow food movement, the "buy local" phenomenon is growing and creating opportunities for social enterprises. The relationship a social enterprise has with its community is a key advantage over private for-profit enterprises, which are sometimes perceived as intruders in the local community. Social enterprises are embedded in their communities. Employees come from the community, and services are often provided to the community. The local nature of the enterprise simplifies the logistics. This was the case for ICR, as it employed local people and provided services for social housing in the community.

The availability and access to potential employees right in the community can also be an advantage. Sectors like construction experience a chronic shortage of trained and skilled workers. Access to potential employees eager to work and train was an advantage to ICR during its start-up and its consequent expansion.

No Profit Leakage

Maintaining surpluses or profits generated by a social enterprise in the company for further capitalization or for distribution to its employees is also an advantage. There are no outside shareholders or owners demanding a share of the profits. In some cases, profits go to support the social programs of related not-for-profit community organizations. In ICR's case, profits generated in the later years paid off existing debt, and the rest remains as equity in the enterprise. In the later years, there has also been a small distribution of profits to the employees. Profit distribution among employees is an opportunity to enhance employee loyalty and increase productivity, thereby making the social enterprise more competitive within the industry.

Availability of Funding Sources

With the increasing awareness of social enterprises and their potential role in the economy, the availability of funding sources increases. Patient capital — low interest loans with long payback periods, critical to the development of social enterprises — is now available from community loan funds across the country. In addition, with the increased awareness about the potential role that social enterprises can play in the alleviation of poverty and other social or environmental problems, granting organizations such as foundations and the United Way have started to support social enterprise development.

Government Deficit as an Opportunity

The recent economic climate can be an opportunity for social enterprises to deliver a service previously provided by government. This may be a result of government dropping a service due to financial constraints or from the realization that a community-based social enterprise is better able to deliver the service. Either way, as discussed in the challenges section, social enterprises need to be aware of government's real intentions on this issue. Is it part of a cost saving or privatization strategy? Despite these concerns, some social enterprises, such as the one established at KidsLink in Ontario, which provides assistance to children with mental health challenges, have entered into and expanded the delivery of social programs.[5]

Economic Impact

There are a number of opportunities for social enterprises to have a bigger role in and impact on the economy. Changing government procurement policies, increasing the scale and size of social enterprises in the economy and pursuing the replication of successful social enterprises are such opportunities.

Public Procurement

Public procurement (the purchase by governments and state-owned enterprises of goods, services and works) accounts for a significant percentage of gross domestic product (GDP) and has a direct impact on the economy. In Canada, government procurement accounts for $14 billion annually, which represents 12–13 percent of GDP.[6] The current commitment by government to tendering all contracts (above $100,000) and obtaining three quotes for contracts between $50,000 and $100,000 as part of their procurement can be prohibitive to social enterprises.

Trade agreements, such as the Agreement on Internal Trade (interprovincial) and the North American Free Trade Agreement (NAFTA), place certain restrictions on procurement practices in Canada. They tend to restrict local preference without reference to social or environmental value, and procurement officials interpret them as meaning that you can't prefer anything other than price and quality. However, small contracts are not subject to trade agreements, which have minimum thresholds, creating an opportunity for small social enterprises. Aboriginal owned-businesses are exempt from trade agreements, which is why the Manitoba provincial government was able to create the Aboriginal Procurement Initiative.

As long as the contracts fall below the thresholds established in free trade agreements, governments can include specific requirements supportive to social enterprises as well as to the community in general into the tendering documents. Such requirements could include employment creation, both in terms of numbers and demographics, delivery of social services and a host of other factors that could advantage social enterprises in accessing government contracts.

These benefits to communities and savings to governments have been recognized in countries such as United Kingdom and Australia. The Scottish government introduced community benefit clauses that provide a means of achieving sustainability in public contracts.[7] They include targeted recruitment and training, small business and social enterprise development and community engagement. Community benefit clauses have been used in construction and social care procurements in Scotland for years.

This concept may require some public political mobilization as the free trade agenda is taking us in the opposite direction. However, if and when the practice of community benefit clauses gets accepted in Canada, they can create significant opportunities for social enterprises across various industry sectors.

Scale and Size

Most social enterprises in Canada are relatively small, in terms of both revenue and number of employees, and this situation is unlikely to change in the foreseeable future.[8] It took ICR eight years to build up to $2 million in annual earned revenue and maintain full-time employment for thirty people. There are, however, some exceptions, like ImagineAbility in Winnipeg, with close to four hundred employees and a fifty-year history, A-Way Express in Toronto, with just under a hundred employees and a twenty-five year history, and the Saskatchewan Association of Rehabilitation Centres (SARC), established in 1968, currently with more than two thousand employees.

In other countries, such as United Kingdom, Italy and Spain, where co-ops are considered social enterprises, very significant scales have been attained. The Mondragon co-ops in Spain, initiated in 1956, have nearly 100,000 employees and billions in earned revenue and are a role model for social enterprises all over the world.[9]

One way to attain size and scale is through replication of successful social enterprises. As long as there is a demand for the product or service in the local market, a successful social enterprise from elsewhere can be replicated, perhaps with modifications. A non-profit organization or any community group concerned with the local economy and social conditions is required to initiate the replication and provide the leadership necessary to get a new enterprise off the ground. The factors fundamental to creating a successful enterprise, such as financing, marketing and a supportive community, need to be present for a replication to succeed.

It can of course be difficult to replicate a successful venture from one location to another. What worked well in one location or at one time may not work in a new place or time. Factors such as relationships with community organizations and funders may need to be modified to fit local realities and market conditions. In theory, the basic ICR business concept of combining employment creation, training and construction services to the non-profit social housing sector can be replicated elsewhere. In fact, there are initiatives in several cities pursuing this concept. The successful Winnipeg-based social enterprise BUILD, which provides energy and water saving retrofits, has already been replicated in St. John's, Newfoundland/Labrador, and Brandon, Manitoba.

There is a general lack of awareness about the emerging role of social enterprises in the Canadian economy, although regional and national advocacy networks are promoting social enterprises as an alternative to private sector corporations. They are trying to educate the general public and to influence policy-makers to develop supportive legislation and government programs. Several universities across the country now offer courses on social enterprise and there is a growing interest in social enterprises by both business and social work students.

There is considerable opportunity for social enterprises in Canada to both increase in numbers and become larger in scale. Once they have developed a critical mass they can play an important role in the economy. Changes in government procurement policies, more public awareness about social enterprises, regional and national networks providing support and more educational programs at Canadian post-secondary schools will all assist in their development.

A More Just and Equal Society

There is a huge opportunity to create a more equalitarian and just society with a significant inclusion of social enterprises in the economy. Much has been documented and written about the effects of a more equal society. Richard Wilkinson and Kate Pickett conducted a number of research projects that illustrate that a more equal society is better for everyone. A significant part of inequality in society, they argue is based on income inequality.[10] We live in a society where some senior executives receive well over five hundred times the pay of their average employee, and the earning gap between top earners and average workers has been increasing.

This widening inequality affects all aspects of a community, ranging from health care, to safety to general well-being and happiness and is responsible for many of society's ills.[11] With their commitment to fair and reasonable wage structures and social justice issues in general, social enterprises are setting a positive example towards decreasing the income inequality gap.

As part of creating a more just and equalitarian society there is also an opportunity for social enterprises to be catalysts to bridge relationships between different cultural groups. One such opportunity exists regarding the relationship between Aboriginal and non-Aboriginal people. Given the history and legacy of colonialism and racism, Aboriginal and non-Aboriginal communities have been skeptical and distrustful of each other for a very long time. This is particularly true in Winnipeg. This mistrust has segregated the communities and helped maintain isolation.

Social enterprises employing both Aboriginal and non-Aboriginal people provide an opportunity for these two groups of employees to both work and socialize together, learn to respect and trust one another. At ICR, non-Aboriginal employees participate in sweats and other traditional Aboriginal ceremonies, while Aboriginal employees participate in activities not part of their traditional culture. Together, they attend funeral ceremonies for loved ones of fellow employees. Together they enjoy leisure and sporting activities. A social enterprise like ICR, with an integrated workforce, has the opportunity to bring the two communities to a closer understanding and appreciation of each other. Bringing people from different cultures and traditions closer together is an opportunity for any social enterprise to help heal some of the rifts, as it did at ICR.

New Economic Paradigm

The current economic system, with high unemployment, persistent poverty and environmental degradation, is not sustainable. The widening gap between the rich and the poor cannot continue. As a society, we could be doing so much better for both people and the environmental sustainability of our planet. There is an opportunity for social enterprises to be transformative and lead the way to a more just society.

Social enterprises can be an integral part of the new economic paradigm, where unemployment is minimized, the disadvantaged are included, workers earn fair wages and benefits and are treated with dignity and respect, and where government and communities have the resources to provide the necessary social services for those in need, while respecting basic rights for everyone.

Social enterprises have been developed not only to provide multiple outcomes — social, environmental and financial — but also to transform the functioning of our economic system. Since the advent of the industrial age, work has by and large been alienating. Work has become focused on maximizing corporate financial goals. This single mindedness has left many individuals on the sidelines, creating the need for social service programs and a safety net for those unable to function in the capitalist paradigm.

There is an opportunity here for an economic model that provides employment with fair wages, good benefits, training and advancement for people currently out of the mainstream. In addition, there is an opportunity to transform work, making it less alienating and more responsive to everyone's social needs. This new paradigm actually has the potential to increase productivity while at the same time humanizing the work place. It has the potential to increase government revenues through taxation and reduce government expenses related to welfare, policing, criminal justice and host of other government services.

Jacques Defourny, Director of the Centre for Social Economy at Liege University in Belgium, puts it this way: social enterprises are a bridge between cooperatives and non-profit organizations since they draw co-ops towards the idea of public service and non-profits towards the idea of production.[12] Building on this concept, there is an opportunity for social enterprises to influence non-profits to become more enterprising and private enterprises become more socially conscious. By being more enterprising, non-profit organizations would be able to support their social goals. I go further and argue that social enterprises can be a bridge between the private for-profit and the not-for-profit sectors, one where private sector corporations include managing for social justice goals, not just maximizing profit, and where the not-for-profit sector is drawn towards the idea of profitable production. At the same time government can assist in these changing roles by formulating appropriate supportive legislation and regulations. At some point in the future, I think there can be — has to be — a time where the distinction between the sectors (private, public and non-profit) is blurred, as they all work towards economic survival and socially just outcomes for everyone.

Notes

1.   <www.unitedwayottawa.ca/what-we-do/investing-in-community/ottawa-community-loan-fund>.
2.   Based on personal conversation with Bill Young (SCP).
3.   SBB 2012.
4.   Young 2008.
5.   <www.kidslinkcares.com>.
6.   OECD 2011.
7.   <www.scotland.gov.uk/Topics/Government/.../procurecombenefits>.
8.   O'Connor et al. 2012.
9.   Based on personal conversations with senior staff during visit to Mondragon, Spain in 2010.
10. Wilkinson and Pickett 2010.
11. Wilkinson and Pickett 2010.
12. Borzaga and Defourny 2001.

Postscript

Since my departure from ICR in 2010, the federal government has introduced several programs to support the role of social enterprises in the Canadian economy and ICR has continued to operate as a successful social enterprise.

In early 2013, the federal government provided $1.5 million to the Trico Charitable Foundation in Calgary to support its Enterprising Non-profits Canada Project. This project provides supports to the network of provincial enterprising non-profits across Canada. On July 3, 2012, the Canadian government issued a news release on improving procurement to benefit the Canadian economy by effectively engaging small and medium enterprises (SMEs), including social enterprises. This federal initiative was preceded in 2011 with a program related to supporting the role of social finance important in the development of social enterprises.

ICR has thrived under my successor John Baker who has taken the company to the next level, increasing both revenue and profitability, while maintaining ICR's commitment to its social mission.

Revenue at July 31, 2012, year-end hit the $3 million mark for the first time, up from $2 million the previous year. Profitability also increased from 1 percent in 2011 to 3 percent in 2012. This compares favourably to the 2010 year-end figures of $2.5 million in revenue and 3.6 percent profit. During this same period, the earned revenue percentage of total revenue increased from 94 percent to 98 percent, reflecting a decrease in grant revenue and an overall increase in total revenue.

The period from 2010 forward has witnessed a significant change in type and size of projects and clients. Residential projects represented 22 percent of the total revenue in 2010 and only 5 percent in 2012. At the same time commercial and institutional projects went from 71 percent of the total revenue in 2010 to 93 percent in 2012. This is a very significant change from 2002, ICR's first year, when the residential sector represented 100 percent of its revenue. This movement illustrates that ICR has been able to adapt to changing conditions and pursue opportunities.

In the period since 2010, ICR entered into major contracts with institutional customers such as Manitoba Housing, University of Winnipeg and Manitoba Hydro. This change to commercial/institutional projects with its slightly higher profit margins and improved productivity resulting from economies of scale are at the core of ICR's improved overall performance.

This change to more institutional and commercial clients required a move to fixed price contracts. Prior to 2011, ICR had successfully negotiated most contracts on a cost-plus basis, thus mitigating major financial risks. Challenges related to fixed price contracts include preparing accurate quotes, mitigating risk related to inflationary pressures on long-term contracts, managing the scope of the projects and negotiating changes to the contract. At the same time quoting on fixed price contracts creates opportunities previously unavailable to ICR as most commercial and institutional projects are based on some form of a fixed price.

Employment at ICR also increased since 2010, peaking at forty-four crew employees. The average number of employees throughout this post 2010 period has been thirty, which is similar to the average rate just before 2010. However, ICR has pursued opportunities that created short-term spikes in the number of employees, all the while maintaining the base number of ICR employees.

ICR has improved on its ratio of target employees. This ratio has increased from approximately 60 percent prior to 2011 to as high as 75 percent, indicating its continuing commitment to its social mission. Changing demographics in the inner city have resulted in more recent immigrants to Canada being employed at ICR. Wages and benefits have also seen advances since 2010. Wage rates reflect those in the construction industry. Benefits, already better than most in the industry, will soon include a pension plan. ICR continues to provide social supports to its employees by tapping into services provided by other community organizations and agencies in the inner city.

ICR continues its commitment to training. There are six ICR employees enrolled in the Manitoba Apprenticeship program, two of whom are entering the fourth and final level before writing the exam for journeyperson status. In addition to its commitment to individuals' skill training, ICR and its staff have been trained and certified for asbestos abatement in confined space work, and it has completed the necessary health and safety training for COR (Certificate of Recognition) certification's first review. The Construction Safety Association of Manitoba has the authority to grant COR certification when a company meets all of the safety requirements.

Currently in its twelfth year, ICR has sustained itself, adapting to market conditions all the while maintaining its commitment to its social mission.

Appendix 1

Executive Summary — ICR Business Plan (April 25, 2002)

Inner City Renovation Inc. is a for-profit enterprise jointly owned by five not-for-profit community development corporations; Community Ownership Solutions Inc. (COS), North End Housing Project (NEHP), Winnipeg Housing and Rehabilitation Corporation (WHRC), Spence Neighbourhood Association (SNA) and West Broadway Development Corporation (WBDC).

The joint venture partners are committed to the following principles related to the new enterprise:

- Hiring the existing renovation workforce previously employed by CEDA as part of its training program.
- Recruiting workers primarily but not exclusively from the three neighbourhoods represented by the community based joint venture partners.
- Hiring at least 25 percent of its workforce from carpentry/construction training program graduates.
- Hiring the majority of its workforce from low-income inner city residents.
- Creating a balance between skilled, semi-skilled and unskilled workers.
- Providing opportunity to its workers to gain skills and access to apprenticeship certification programs.
- Providing employee ownership and participatory management training to all employees of the enterprise.
- Creating employee ownership in the new enterprise once it is stable having completed two successive profitable years.
- Sourcing and flowing through skills training funds as required.
- Creating a board of directors with representatives from the joint venture partners as well as outside directors with skills related to the construction sector.
- Creating board seats for staff representatives.

The enterprise provides construction/renovation services mainly but not limited to not-for-profit housing development organizations. The enterprise is scheduled to start operations in July 2002. It will have 20 full-time employees at time of start-up and employment is expected to increase to 38 full-time staff by the end of year one. Projected net income for year one is just above breakeven at $22,800. The income statement takes into consideration that the general manager's salary will be paid by COS for the first six months starting one month before the official enterprise start-up. Incorporation and all legal fees will also be paid for by COS. In addition the enterprise will receive a $50,000 grant from COS. The enterprise will need to establish a $100,000 line of credit with a financial institution.

The joint venture partners are committed to provide a minimum of $476,000 in renovation contracts in the first year and greater volumes in subsequent years. This will go a long way to reducing financial risks.

The enterprise will provide average or better industry wages and benefits for its workers, opportunities for skill development, career advancement and potential employee ownership.

Appendix 2

ICR Timeline

April 2002	Community Ownership Solutions (COS) completes business plan for a construction social enterprise.
June 2002	Incorporates as a share capital corporation.
June 2002	Wins the Social Capital Partners (SCP) national business-plan competition.
August 2002	Starts up with six shareholders (COS, SCP, North End Housing Project, West Broadway Community Development Corporation, Spence Neighbourhood Association and Partners for Housing).
September 2002	Completes the first residential renovation project for North End Housing Project.
June 2003	Moves out of the COS downtown offices to its own location on Dufferin Avenue in Winnipeg's North End.
May 2004	Grand opening of Urban Circle training Centre, ICR's first commercial project.
October 2004	First weekend retreat for ICR staff and family held at Maskwa Project near Pine Falls.
November 2004	Redeems the shares held by three shareholders (Spence Neighbourhood Association, West Broadway Community Development Corporation and Partners for Housing).
September 2005	Wins CIAO Magazine Kitchen Award
November 2005	Move to a larger space on Jarvis Avenue.
December 2005	Restructures and changes legal name to Inner City Development Inc. (ICD) to accommodate the start-up of new business units. ICR continues to operate as a division of ICD.
January 2006	Inner city Janitorial (ICJ) and Inner City Property Management (ICPM) start-up as new business units of ICD.
January 2006	Initiation of payroll deposit as well as employee savings program
April 2006	Completion of first residential infill project (Alexander Street)
April 2006	Sets up new safety committee and work commences on a company safety manual.
May 2006	Starts relationship with Housing Opportunities Program (HOP).
July 2006	Posts first profitability at year-end and pays corporate income tax. Income statement includes grant revenue without which ICR would have incurred a loss for the year.

November 2006	Initiates the first new build commercial building project (ACU branch on north Main Street).
December 2006	ICPM property manager resigns and existing property management contracts are terminated. ICPM ceases to operate.
January 2007	Enters into relationship with Yarrow Sash and Door as dedicated installer.
April 2007	Retained by BridgmanCollaborative Architecture as project manager for the renovations and additions to the Dominion Bank Building at Higgins Avenue and Main Street.
May 2007	ICD Board decides to close down ICJ. After 17 months of operation ICJ was unable to reach economy of scale necessary to compete in this sector.
June 2007	Contributes to renovations of Wesley Hall (University of Winnipeg) and the historic HEAP Building on Portage Avenue.
July 2007	Celebrates 5th anniversary with a bus tour highlighting 22 ICR completed projects in the inner city. Ninety people attend the celebration including representatives from all three levels of government.
August 2007	Releases "Rebuilding Winnipeg's North End," a DVD produced by the Cooperators Insurance Company.
November 2007	General Manager nominated for the Shwab Foundation Canadian Social Entrepreneur of the Year award, part of a global competition.
December 2007	North End Housing Project redeems its shares. SCP and COS remain as equal shareholders.
January 2008	Brian Pollock successfully completes the apprenticeship training program and becomes first ICR employee to complete course from start to finish and obtain the red seal journeyperson carpenter designation.
February 2008	Moves existing houses on University of Winnipeg new site for the Richardson Building elsewhere on vacant lots in the neighbourhood and restores them.
April 2008	Completes its first "green" residential renovation complete with a green roof garden.
May 2008	Management and supervisory staff complete eleven-session custom management training course.
May 2008	Establishes a relationship with Lowe Mechanical and enters into contract to retrofit 150 units in a nursing home.
June 2008	Nominated for Manitoba Excellence in Sustainability Awards.
October 2008	Chosen as the "Employer of the Year" by Apprenticeship Manitoba.
November 2008	Completes new ACU branch on Pembina Highway. Project completed to Gold LEED standard.

March 2009	Completes phase one of the *Ahsanook* project for Southern First Nations Network of Care.
September 2009	Brian Pollock nominated for Manitoba journey person of the year is chosen as runner up.
July 2009	Enters into relationship with MacDonald Youth Services.
November 2009	Charity Intelligence Canada recognizes ICR as one of four social enterprises in Canada and recommends ICR for financial support.
April 2010	Donates $500 to the 2010 Special Olympics Manitoba Team to support ICR employee who was selected to the Manitoba bowling team.
May 2010	SCP redeemed their 50% share in ICR leaving COS as the sole shareholder.
July 2010	I retire and John Baker starts as the new General Manager.

Appendix 3

ICR Recognition

During its first ten years, ICR was recognized as a leader in the social enterprise sector. It received numerous awards and was featured on both local and national television, and in newspapers and journals.

Awards

Oct. 2005	ICR receives the Ciao Kitchen Design/Renovation award for a private residential addition and kitchen renovation.
Oct. 2008	The Manitoba Apprenticeship and Certification Board recognizes ICR as the "Employer of the Year" for its commitment to apprenticeship training in Manitoba.
Nov. 2008	Runner up in the business category of the Manitoba Excellence in Sustainability Awards.
Oct. 2009	ICR employee Brian Pollock, a journeyperson carpenter, is a finalist in the journeyperson of the year awards presented by the Manitoba Apprenticeship and Certification Board.
Nov. 2009	One of four social enterprises across Canada and the only one in Manitoba recommended by Charity Intelligence Canada.

Media

ICR has received recognition in the print, audio and visual media. Numerous articles have appeared in the local Winnipeg newspapers. CBC, CTV and Shaw Cable featured ICR in various television programs, and CBC radio has also provided coverage on its local Winnipeg morning broadcast. Construction trade journals, community economic development journals and community newsletters have featured articles on ICR over the years.

Television

Feb. 29, 2004	CBC *Venture* features Social Capital Partners and ICR.
March 29, 2004	Shaw Cable in Manitoba produces an original feature on ICR.
Oct. 26, 2007	CTV covers ICR's five-year anniversary celebration.
June 30, 2009	CBC National feature on "Making Canada Proud."

Radio

March 29, 2004	CBC Information Radio (local Winnipeg broadcast) interviews ICR's general manager.

Newspapers

Sept. 20, 2002	"Inner city renovation firm builds a future for people," *Winnipeg Free Press*.
Feb. 5, 2004	"Go-Slow approach pays off for Inner City Renovation," *Winnipeg Free Press*.
Feb. 17, 2006	"Work faster, work harder. Job tips for deep freeze," *Winnipeg Sun*.
May 8, 2006	"Employers Head to Jail for Job Forum," *Winnipeg Free Press*.
June 2006	"Building a future, Company gives workers a shot," *Winnipeg Sun*.
Feb. 17, 2008	"Doomed Homes Live Again," *Winnipeg Free Press*.
May 2, 2009	"Building inner-city hope one vital job at a time," *Winnipeg Free Press*.
Aug. 30, 2010	"Inner-city job project cuts welfare costs, turns profit, Group tallies social benefits," *Winnipeg Free Press*.
Nov. 4, 2011	"The Business of Creating Meaning," *The Globe and Mail*.

Journals

Summer 2009	"Inner City Development Inc., More than Just Construction," *The CA Executive Journal*.
Winter 2009	"Winnipeg Construction Company Focuses on Financial, Social and Environmental beneficence," *Canadian Builders Quarterly*.
Summer 2009	"Marketing Social Enterprise," Glen Lougheed and Marty Donkervoort, *Making Waves*.

Appendix 4

Social Return on Investment

Inner City Renovation
Community Based
Residential & Commercial Construction
Inner City Renovation: Social Mission Overview

Goals

- Hire majority of ICR employees from low-income, inner city neighbourhoods
- Contribute to the revitalization of Winnipeg's inner city
- Provide 'quality' jobs to target employee group
- Provide opportunities for skill development and internal career laddering
- Establish an ICR employee ownership plan once the enterprise has stabilized and reached profitability

Methods

- Recruit at least 60% of employees from low-income, inner city neighborhoods
- Dedicate significant proportion of contract opportunities to inner city projects
- Pay market wages and employee benefits
- Establish apprenticeship program, participatory management training and career laddering structure
- Retain Employee Social Support Worker
- Develop employee steering committees and regular staff social and educational events

Success Metrics

- ICR maintains a 60% employee average from the target population
- Current and past target employees are able to lessen or eliminate need for government financial assistance
- Tangible progress made regarding individual target employee sustainable livelihood asset development
- ICR retains majority of target employees while reaching profitability

SROI Report Card: Year End Jully 31, 2003*

Financial Performance	
Total Sales Revenue	$935,000
Total Grants and Subsidies	$115,000
Total Sales Revenue and Grants	$1,150,000
Total Operating Profit (Loss)	$(245,000)
Additional Social Support Infrastructure	$8,000
Total Investment Required to Date	$368,000

Social Return On Investment	
Average Change in Societal Contribution (Target Employees)	$13,600
Average Number of Target Employees	18.5
Total Change in Societal Contribution	$149,500
Ongoing Portion of Societal Contribution	$74,000
One Year SROI	41%
Annuity Multiplier	12
Projected Long Term SROI	241%

Overview of Business

- Renovation and construction company committed to the revitalization of Winnipeg's inner city residential housing and creating quality employment for low-income, inner city residents
- The company was started as a joint venture between five nonprofits committed to inner city renewal
- Business provides full service renovations to both residential and commercial customers in the inner city of Winnipeg
- The vision is to move the company into an employee ownership business model after ICR has reached two consecutive years of profitability

Sustainable Livelihoods Outcomes

- Improved social connectedness through staff retreats and off-sites
- Employee social committee has been created as first step toward participative management
- Staff have 24/7 access to crisis councilor
- Employee wages average $12.75/hr compared to $6.75 minimum wage
- Most employees use bank accounts rather than cheque cashing services

- Only 5% of staff continue to use food banks and frequency has dropped
- $2,000 invested in basic tools and safety equipment for target employees
- Partnership created with local College for journeyman training

Overview of Target Population

- 79% unemployed before ICR employment
- 60% receiving social assistance before ICR employment
- 90% male
- Majority are Aboriginal
- 11% high school graduates
- 58% have criminal record
- 37% had ever held a job for no more than 2 years
- 63% have dependent children
- 47% needed food bank services in the year prior to ICR employment
- Few had bank accounts at hire — most used cheque cashing services

Employment Outcomes

- Provided full time jobs for 26 individuals throughout yr 1
- Peak employment of 19 individuals
- Paid approx. C$480K in wages to target employees
- Generated approx. C$67K in income tax from target employees
- Experienced annualized employee turnover of 52%
- Organized workforce into teams of 1 tradesmen and 2 target employees
- Experienced ongoing challenges with attendance and productivity which contributed to financial losses
- Turnover stabilized by end of year
- HR policies and employee handbook created

* SROI reports were done annually from 2003–2009, other than 2006–07 which was done as a two-year report. Also, the SROI reports for all years, 2003–2009, are available on the ICR website as a pdf at SROI ICR Report Card 2003 –2009 <http://www.innercityrenovation.ca/about.php>.

SROI Report Card: Year End July 31, 2009

Financial Performance	
Total Sales Revenue:	$1,509,963
Total Grants and Subsidies	$56,910
Total Sales Revenue and Grants	$1,566,873
Total Operating Profit (Loss)	$108,026
Additional Social Support Infrastructure	$6,700
Total Investment for Year Seven	$63,610
Total Investment Required to Date	$1,339,135

Social Return On Investment	
Average Change in Societal Contribution (Target Employees)	$6,381
Average Number of Target Employees	12
Number of Target employees in Sample Group	12
Current Year Cost Savings to Society	$76,569
Cumulative Cost Savings (to 2008)	$664,567
Total Cost Savings to Date	$741,136
Cumulative SROI	55%

Overview of Business

- Revenues increased by 9.8%
- Profit has contributed to reducing the accumulated deficit
- Completed more than 255 projects since start-up
- Generated more than $9.3 million in earned revenue since start-up
- Paid out nearly $4 million in wages and benefits to its employees

Sustainable Livelihoods Outcomes

- Four target employees were registered in the Apprenticeship Carpentry training program
- Two employees took a project management course
- ICR continues to provide a social calendar of events in order to encourage social connections for staff and their families e.g., sporting & recreational events, staff Christmas party, family picnic etc.
- Employees have indicated that they feel they are getting along better with others as a result of their employment with ICR

Overview of Target Population

- 60% Aboriginal
- Average age is 40
- 33% of original target employee base recruited in Year 1 are still with ICR
- Hired employee with a disability (intellectual) that has worked with current employees

Employment Outcomes

- Maintained average 60% target/non target employee ratio throughout Year seven
- Average target employee wage of $15.75 and average hourly wage for all staff of $16.50 over the past year which is $6.75 more than minimum wage
- This wage increase for target employees is a 1.6% increase over the average wage calculated in 2008
- Target employees continue to enjoy their work at ICR and most view ICR as a good career opportunity
- Long-term employees noted an improvement in their technical skills

Definitions and Methodology

Total Investment Required to Date • Represents all cash injections in the business	Total operating losses + Grants and Subsidies + Additional Support Infrastructure = Total Investment Required
Change in Societal Contribution (Target Employees) • Difference between the direct societal "cost" or "benefit" contributed by the employee before hire versus after hire	Annual Social Assistance Before Hire - Annual Income Tax Paid Before Hire + Annual Income Tax Paid After Hire = Change in Societal Contribution
Ongoing Portion of Societal Contribution • The component of the change in financial position that can be measured beyond year one	Annual Income Tax Paid After Hire - Annual Income Tax Before Hire = Ongoing Portion of Societal Contribution
Annuity Multiplier • Projected value of ongoing new income tax contributions generated by target employee in the future	
Current Year SROI • Return on investment generated by the current year change in target employee financial position	Total Change in Societal Contribution / Total Investment Required =Current Year SROI
Projected Long Term SROI • SROI generated by extrapolating the ongoing portion of the change in employee financial position into the future	Ongoing Portion of Societal Contribution * Annuity Multiplier / Total investment Required =Projected Long Term SROI

Data Gathering Process

- Target employees are interviewed to obtain a baseline socioeconomic data
- Data is gathered regarding employment and sustainable livelihood status prior at hire
- A second survey is taken at the end of each year to determine changes for target employees
- Only target employees who are employed for more than three months are considered for SROI calculations

References

Ben-Shahar, Tal. 2007. *Happier: Learn the Secrets to Daily Joy and Lasting Fulfillment*. New York: McGraw-Hill.

Borzaga, Carlo, and Jacques Defourny. 2001. *The Emergence of Social Enterprises*. London: Routledge.

CCPA-MB (Canadian Centre for Policy Alternatives-Manitoba). 2006. *Inner-City Voices, Community-Based Solutions: State of the Inner City Report, 2006*. Winnipeg: Canadian Centre for Policy Alternatives-Manitoba.

Chantier de l'economie Sociale. 2008. "À propos de nous: Mission et mandats." At <chantier.qc.ca>.

Comack, Elizabeth, and Jim Silver. 2006. *Safety and Security Issues in Winnipeg's Inner City Communities: Bridging the Community-Police Divide*. Ottawa: Canadian Centre for Policy Alternatives.

CPWR (Center for Construction Research and Training). 2007. *The Construction Chart Book*, fourth edition. Silver Spring, MD: CPWR.

Deane, Lawrence. 2006. *Under One Roof — Community Economic Development and Housing in the Inner City*. Winnipeg and Black Point, NS: Fernwood Publishing.

Defourny, Jacques, and Marthe Nyssens. 2008. "Social Enterprises in Europe: Recent Trends and Development." WP No 08/01, European Research Network (EMES). At <www.emes.net/fileadmin/emes/PDF>.

ENP (Enterprising Non-Profits Program). 2010. *The Canadian Social Enterprise Guide*. Vancouver: Enterprising Non-Profits Program.

Gonzales, Vanna. 2010. "Italian Social Co-operatives and the Development of Civic Capacity: A Case of Co-operative Renewal?" *Affinities* 4, 1.

Kardash, Nancy, and Jim Mochoruk. 2000. *The People's Co-op: The Life and Times of a North End Institution*. Winnipeg and Black Point, NS: Fernwood Publishing.

Loughheed, Glen, and Marty Donkervoort. 2009. "Marketing Social Enterprise." *Making Waves* 20, 2.

MacFarlane, Richard, and Mark Cook. 2008. *Community Benefits in Public Procurement*. Edinburgh: The Scottish Government. At <scotland.gov.uk/Publications/2008/02/13140629/0>.

O'Connor, Ryan, Peter Elson, Peter Hall and Brendan Reimer. 2012. *Measuring the Size, Scope and Scale of the Social Enterprise Sector in Manitoba*. Winnipeg: The Canadian CED Network. At <ccednet-rcdec.ca/en/node/10481>.

OECD (Organization of Economic Cooperation and Development). 2011. "Size of Public Procurement Market." *Government at a Glance 2011*. Directorate for Public Governance and Territorial Development. At <oecd.org/gov/governmentataglance2011.htm>.

___. 2009. "OECD Principles for Integrity in Public Procurement." At <www.oecd.org>.

Quarter, Jack, Laurie Mook and Ann Armstrong. 2009. *Understanding the Social Economy: A Canadian Perspective*. Toronto: University of Toronto Press.

Roy, Arun S., and Ging Wong. 2000. "Direct Job Creation Programs: Evaluation Lessons on Cost-Effectiveness." *Canadian Public Policy/Analyse de Politiques* XXVI, 2.

Silver, Jim. 2012. "Persistent Poverty in Canada." In Les Samuelson and Wayne

Antony (eds.), *Power and Resistance* fifth edition. Winnipeg and Black Point, NS: Fernwood Publishing.

SBB (Small Business Branch), Industry Canada. 2012. *Key Small Business Statistics*.

Wilkinson, Richard, and Kate Pickett. 2010. *The Spirit Level: Why Equality is Better for Everyone*. London: Penguin Books.

Young, Bill. 2008. *The Five Critical Factors of Social Enterprise Profitability*. At <www. socialcapitalpartners.ca/ideas-learning>.

Index